# His Word Made Manifest

Jaclyn O. Chukwuocha

authorHOUSE®

*AuthorHouse™*
*1663 Liberty Drive*
*Bloomington, IN 47403*
*www.authorhouse.com*
*Phone: 1 (800) 839-8640*



*Published by AuthorHouse 04/20/2015*

*ISBN: 978-1-5049-0611-1 (sc)*
*ISBN: 978-1-5049-0610-4 (e)*

*Print information available on the last page.*

# Contents

# Foreword

There is no doubt that we are in perilous times according to 2 Timothy 3:1 which says that in the last days perilous times shall come. Unfortunately, the body of Christ that should uphold, effect discipline and appropriateness of God's word and mandate are in slumber. There is no doubt that the world is in the church, and the church is in the world. Time has come for believers, to **heed** God's warning not to love the world, as in 1 John 2:15.

This state has prompted Sis Jackie to write this book. I pray that revival will start in your hearts even as you peruse this book. I prophesy that the words of God in this book will transform and affect you positively. Not only shall you read, you will receive grace to apply the it to your lives.

Any time the church returns to the word of God, there is always a revival. In the days of King Josiah in II Kings chapters 22 and 23, the book of the law was found in the house of the Lord and handed over to the King and when he read it, the result was repentance accompanied by revival. The disciples said "But we will give ourselves continually to prayer and to THE MINISTRY OF THE WORD" (Acts

6:4), and the outcome was explosive. Apart from the increase in the number of the disciples, there was revival among the religious people of the day, and the bible says, "...... a great company of the priests were obedient to the faith".

Revival tarries today because the church of God. Though knowledge is increasing according to prophecy but the value placed upon the word and the love of many for the same are growing cold; but God is issuing out a call for His people to return back to His word and His commandments and walk by them.

This is what this book "His Word Made Manifest" has come to do. It will encourage and motivate you to return back to the word of God.

I recommend it, I have gone through it and it provoked a desire in me for more of His word.

May God's word, richly profit and bless you. Be blessed as you read.

Pastor (Dr) Toyin Laoye
Senior Pastor,
RCCG, Dominion Cathedral,
Orange NJ.

# Introduction

God's word is eternal even as God is, there will never be a time that there shall be no need of God's word in our lives. And without doubt the word of God is made manifest in every ramification of man's life. To a great extent, it is the only balm that heals every of man's wound- assuring, soothing and protective. And with the dramatic turn of world's event, every life and particularly Christians cannot do without this one and only solution. Jesus told His followers.

***"---- the words that I speak unto you,***
***they are spirit and they are life".***
***(John 6:63).***

The word of God is an inevitable life-source for man on planet earth. It is so because the bible is simply God printed on letters, and God is life and the only author of every of everything that lives. Any one who desires to make it in life must partner with the living word. It is the manifestation of the word of God that results in fulfilled destinies and purposes. I must warn here that, having the word of God is more than buying an expensive bible and giving it a room in your shelf as furniture. Many have made this a habit, they have the most fanciful and costly bibles on their shelves while their lives are striking contradictions to the demands and commands of the scriptures.

Quite fortunately, some have died physically or spiritually where as they have the source of life within their reach.

The scripture reveals that we are in the perilous days of planet earth, implying the earth may not get better.

***"This know also, that in the last days perilous times shall come". (2 Timothy 3:1-7).***

But as it was in Genesis chapter one, it is only a word from God that can make a difference. Only God's word can bring an end to formless situations of the last days. Strictly speaking, it is only those who make the word of God their companion that shall make a difference. Those that know their God trust in and walk by His words shall do exploits, they shall manifest the living word.

***"If ye know these things, happy are ye if ye do them". (John 13:1).***

You will never regret a partnership with God's word. The result will be a fulfilled and happy life as God's word is made manifest daily in everything you do and say. Have a nice and refreshing time with His word.

## Chapter One

# MANIFEST AS TRUTH

As Christians, the word of God is pivotal to our daily living, it is an information and power source for life's journey. From the word of God, man discovers and understands his origin and being. Man's destiny is packaged and concealed in it. The person of God and man's relationship with God is revealed in the scriptures. The word of God bears the authentic record of man's history and his dispensational encounters with his maker, it holds the unchallengeable truth that man needs for survival and progress.

From the word of God we discover, and we believe that God created all things and by His own power. It is also a biblical truth that God sent His son, Jesus Christ to die in our place and atone for our sins. We further acknowledge the truth that for our sake too, God has given the Holy Spirit as a senior partner and helper in every situation of life. These three personalities-God the father, God the son and God the Holy Spirit, are directly linked to all that pertains to man. Our lives evolve around God and His unfailing word. The truthfulness of God and His word is one attribute that demarcates and differentiates God from man. The truthfulness of God's word draws a bold line between God and us.

The conspicuous border between the word of God and that of man is emphasized in the scriptures. Hence the book of ***Numbers 23:19*** states clearly,

***"God is not a man, that He should lie, Neither the son of man that he should repent Hath he said and shall He not do it? Or hath He spoken And shall he not make it good?***

God's word is not the word of man and cannot by any measure be compared to the word of man. Men change their minds and therefore break their words; they lie, because they repent. But God does neither, He never changes His mind, and therefore never withdraws His promises. Man can promise a thing and fail to it but when God says a thing that which He says must come to pass. Such is the imperfection of man and such the perfection of God. It is impossible for God to lie. The word of God represents God Himself. This indeed is a heart warming truth that with God, there is neither variableness nor shadow of turning.

The more reason every child of God should allow the word of God to detect and direct every step made in life's journey. The disappointing fact though, is that some so called Christians, filled with the Holy Spirit and tongue talking, live in doubt of the word of God. Though they read the bible daily and listen to the word of God preached and taught during weekly church activities, when it comes to the manifestation of the truth in the word of God they have reservations. Can we think otherwise of God than that He is unchangeable, and all His promises inviolable. As children of God our faith on the unfailing word of God should be unfailing. But should we choose to act otherwise, our infidelity and obstinacy cannot invalidate or overthrow the truthfulness of God's word.

***"God forbid: yea let God be true,***
***but every man a liar; as it is written,***
***That thou mightest be justified in***
***Thy sayings: And mightest overcome***
***When thou art judged" (Romans 3:4).***

God's word must be accomplished, His purposes performed and all His ends answered, though there be generation that by their unbelief go about to make God a liar. God is true to every word which He has spoken, and will let none of it fall to the ground. We had better question and overthrow the credit of all the men in the world including you, than doubt the faithfulness of God.

For all men are fickle and mutable, and given to change, vanity and lie. But God does and will continue to preserve His own honor upon the earth, notwithstanding the unfaithfulness of men.

Why it might seem that things are not working out for you is because you are yet to discover or locate what God says about your situation. See, you are not to believe and accept what man says about your situation, man does not have the final say, God does. People might advice you on certain issues but only God holds the key that can unlock that situation and that key is in His word.

As much as I agree that God can use man to fulfill His promises in our lives, the fact also remains that every spirit filled child of God should be sensitive to realize when the words of men attempts to challenge the unchangeable word of God over our situation.

We should know when what we are given is off the track of God's word. Your spirit man should be able to detect the right word from that which is wrong. No word of man can supercede or invalidate the truthfulness of God's word. God's word is final because it is infallibly the truth.

There is only one universally recognized liar-Satan the devil. He is the opposite of truth and the originator, and manufacturer of lies and therefore qualifies as father of them that reject the truth. Jesus tags them "children of the devil".

***"Ye are of your father the devil and***
***the lusts of your father ye will do He***
***was a murderer from the beginning***
***And abode not in the truth, Because***
***There is no truth in him. When he***
***Speaketh a lie he speaketh of his own***
***For he is a liar, and the father of it.***
***(John 8:44)***

Any one who tells you anything contrary to God's word is of the devil, for the devil is the only one that carries the nature and habit of lies. So when you receive God's word and someone comes around with something contrary, sowing a seed of doubt then you should discover the devil is trying to trick you. Don't forget one of his cardinal missions against us;

***"The thief cometh not, but for to steal -------"***
***(John 10:10)***

And that includes the word of God in your life. He has nothing good to offer you. Yet, he will not leave you alone. He is always there to manifest his destructive tendencies. You might resist him now and the next moment he is back. Are you surprise he behaves this way? You should recall he carries a battered head; his head was bruised by the seed of the woman, so he cannot reason properly.

## ARE YOU GOING TO ALLOW HIM?

Never. You have to determine not to allow him ruin your life as his. That is why Apostle Paul commands;

***"Watch ye, stand fast in the faith,***
***quit you like men, be strong"***
***(1 Cor. 16:13).***

You have to be alert and on your guard, keep your ground and abide in the inspired word of God and do not give it up for anything, not for the wisdom of this world, nor suffer it to be corrupted by it. Stand by faith on the word of God, maintain it even to death, do not forsake the profession it and yield to its influence.

Show yourself a child of God by your steadiness, sound judgment and firm resolution. Do not stagger in your faith. We are not to be moved by any wind that blows our way in form of words, else we'll be blown to the point of no return.

When God instructed the first man and woman on the forbidden tree the devil saw instability in the woman and decided to blow her away with the wind of falsehood.

***"Yea, hath God said ye shall not eat of every tree of the garden?" (Gen. 3:1)***

You can agree with me that God did not tell them not to eat of every tree of the garden; it was only one particular tree that He commanded them not to eat. The devil himself knows the truth but being a trickster, he questioned her with a negative aim. And unfortunately he achieved his aim. He found Eve, a channel to use because he sought for a fragile heart with a fragile faith. Eve was deceived because she chose not to stand fast in the word of God. Instead of abiding on the truth of God's word, she succumbed to the lies of the devil. And this is common in Christendom today.

Some believers find it hard to believe what God says concerning their situations. They prefer the lies that seem to resemble the truth due to impatience. Impatience has put a lot of Christians off the track to their own shame and loss. When God says a thing, just be rest assured that it shall surely come to pass. If God says a thing, the next thing that follows is the fulfillment, no matter how long it takes; there can be no change of mind. So if God says you are blessed, swallow it as He has said it, believe it and work upon it because He has control over all the situations of your life.

Look at this from this perspective, should the president of your country instructs that you be promoted, I guess what you will do next, will be to rejoice and prepare for that promotion and the abundance it will attract. Now, the word of the president is the word of man, who is limited in the capacity of executing his word, but you will rejoice because the number one man has spoken on your situation and you trust that it will be carried out.

Today, the one greater than your president is sending a heart warming letter of promotion to you through His word. Why can't you rejoice and do away with doubt and unbelief? Let's consider this for instance, the word of God says:

***"There shall nothing cast their young, nor be barren in thy land, the number of thy days I will fulfill" (Exodus 23:26).***

God is saying that the thing that cut people's life short even at their prime shall not be powerful enough to cut short your life when it is not according to God's timing. After reading this, I guess you should go to sleep; be rest assured that untimely death is erased from your forehead.

This letter has a direct bearing with Christian sisters, the reason I will suggest they read it meditatively to absorb the yeast of it. A lot of Christian sisters have messed themselves up in the hands of herbalists and fake prophets, seeking the fruit of the womb. But for you, the word of God is saying today, that you will not be barren. So believe the word of God and do not doubt or argue with God because of how long you have waited.

That you have been married for years (no matter how long) does not make God a liar. God is God and His word is truth. Wait for the manifestation of the power of His word in your life, wait and you will testify of God's faithfulness.

King David in one of his psalms says he meditates on the law of God all day long because he loves it. God has given us His word to meditate on always. David, a man after God's heart held unwaveringly on the truthfulness of God's word ***(Psalms 119: 142, 151).***

Now, check your life, is there any area of your life you can recall you have been a proof of the truthfulness of God's word? Or are you allowing the devil to reduce your life to that of mediocrity because of doubt? Are you a Christian who swallows the devil's trash and gives up to fate? You should have a choice, "anything" should not go for you but only what God says.

What are you doing with God's word? Do you know God is ready to change and repair what the devil has destroyed, just by His word? God has given His word to you on purpose, to put in order what the enemy has disorganized. If you decide to keep quiet, God will do nothing. But if you act on His word, speaking it into your situation, God will intervene because He honors His word. What you believe and confess is bound to manifest in your life. Christianity is more than a religion, it is life and must be lived to the fullest.

God desires that your life remains a living testimony of the truthfulness of His word. Your life is supposed to be an epistle, a mirror that reflects the beauty of the Lord. As a Christian, if you carry and walk in God's goodness, it will affirm assuredly the truthfulness of God's word. The word of God is to manifest, show off on you that the almighty be glorified. If as Christians we cannot display the truthfulness of God's word, what other proves do we have before the unbelievers.

***Romans 8:19*** says the world is waiting for you to manifest the truthfulness of God's word and you have no option but live up to God's demand.

Remember, it is the amount of God's word manifested in your life that credits you a true and worthy witness and attracts others to Christ. I pray that the truth of God's word shall be continually manifested in your life. Amen.

## Chapter Two

# MANIFEST AS IMMUTABLE

The immutability of God's word implies that the word of God is not subject to change; it cannot change but remains what it is. Right from the beginning of things, it is God's word that was instrumental to the creation of what now is from nothingness. The heavens and the earth were created through the word of God and the immutable word is still an instrument, an avenue through which what was not is brought to be:

***"For this they willingly are ignorant of, that by the word of God, the heavens were of old, and The earth standing out of the water And in the water" (2 Pet. 3:5).***

Though men might know of the immutability of the word of God and ought to have known it, yet this they willingly are ignorant of. They choose to pass it over in silence as if they had never heard or known anything of it. If they knew it, they did not like to retain it in their knowledge; they did not care to own it. And it is hard to persuade men to believe what they are not willing to find time for. They are ignorant because they are willing to be ignorant and they do not know because they do not care to know. Yet that in any case does not invalidate the truth that God's word is immutable. From the bible we discover that the heavens and the earth and their fullness were created by the word of God. The word has ever and will always be; nothing can be removed or added to it.

***"Heaven and earth shall pass away***
***But my word shall not pass away"***
***(Luke 21:33).***

God Himself is saying that heaven and earth shall pass away sooner than any word of His. His word will take effect and not one of them falls to the ground. Though the heavens and the earth were created by the word of God, they will surely pass away but the word of God shall endure forever. The word of God is steadfast, it cannot change. Most believers have ended up as failures because of their ignorance of the immutability of God's word. As long as success is concerned the knowledge of God's word is not negotiable. Many have lost out in the race of life and success.

**WHY?**

To them the word of God has become obsolete and powerless. They know it too well and are tired of repeating the same thing everyday. They wish there could be new sermons, new stories, new parables, and new prophecies. How long will they continue to hear that Jesus is coming soon? When is soon? Questions of this sort have made some doubt the word of God. They think and try to convince themselves and others to believe that the bible is just a book some old folks put together and give a name-the bible. But the bible is more than a book, it is a book of books, it is the very word of God delivered to man. As I have already stated, it is God Himself printed in letters.

***"For the prophecy came not in old by the will of man but holy men of God spake as they were moved by the Holy Ghost" (2 Pet. 1:21).***

***"All scriptures is inspired of God, and is profitable for doctrine, for reproof, for Correction, for instruction in righteousness. That the man of God may be perfect thoroughly furnished unto all good works" (2 Tim. 3:16-17)***

The word of God came not by the will or decision of men, nor the will of any of the prophets or penmen of the scriptures. It is the reason why any of those things were written makes up the canon of the scripture. But holy men of God spoke as they were moved by the Holy Ghost. The Holy Ghost is the supreme agent; the holy men are but instruments.

A comparison of the two scriptures above reveals that the Holy ghost inspired and dictated to the writers of the scriptures what they were to deliver of the mind of God. It is the Holy Spirit that powerfully excited and effectually engaged these holy men to speak (and write what He had put into their mouths). The Holy Ghost also wisely and carefully assisted and directed them in the delivery of what they had received from Him. Such that they were completely free of the least mistake in expressing what He revealed to them.

Implying that the very words of the Bible are to be received and counted as the very words of the Holy Ghost and as proceeding from God. This is the reason we must esteem and reverence the bible, for every jot of it expresses the mind of God for us. The word of God is meant for our own good. As for God, He is comfortable in heaven, He has never been reported sick or oppressed or anything of such. He knew we will need His word to counter the plans of the devil that is why He inspired men to pen down His words. If we then learn to take Him by His word, it will profit us and work for our good. God's word is immutable. He says,

***"For I am the Lord, I change not, therefore ye sons of Jacob are not consumed (Malachi 3:6)***

Here we have God's immutability asserted by Him. He does not change; therefore no word that He has spoken shall fall to the ground. A practical proof of God's immutability is the comfortable experience the Israelites had of Him.

They had every reason to testify that God is unchangeable because God remained faithful to His covenant with them and their fathers. If not for His immutability, they would have been consumed and long cut off from being a people.

They had been false and fickle in their conduct to Him. God would have just abandoned them to their ruin but because He remembers His covenant and would not violate nor alter the thing that had gone out of His lips, they were preserved from ruin. It was purely because He is as good as His word. His word will never change and He Himself cannot change.

As long as God cannot change, then we can be sure His word will not change, it abides for ever. And accepting Christ means in essence accepting His word as truth. We cannot profess to accept Christ and not His word; His word cannot be separated from Him. If we have accepted him as the Lord of our lives, we must automatically accept His word as the guide for our daily lives.

We should be able to draw a line between the word of God and that of Man. When men speak and claim they have spoken of God, we should be able to test the authenticity of such words with the written word of God. The word of God is indeed immutable but the word of man is not. I can testify to the immutability of God's word. There are circumstances in life that have brought me to a point where I had to hold on to the word of God.

There was a time in my life that I made a move that of my own, I couldn't have succeeded. The only thing that kept me on was the immutable word of God. Despite contrary advice not to, His word pushed me on. This move of course had to do with traveling to a strange country where I had no body to call a family member. The word I held onto is,

***"The earth is the Lords and the fullness thereof the world, and the that dwell therein" (Psalms 24:1).***

I held onto this word of God and kept praying with it, until I was convinced by the spirit of God to go ahead. You see, what gave me the boldness to get back to God was His word, declaring Him as the owner of all the nations of the world and my firm belief that He could see me through, probably you may find yourself in a similar situation and your mind may make you feel God is far away in heaven separated from the earth. I want you to know that all the parts and regions of the earth are the Lord's, all under His eye, all in His hands, so that wherever a child of God goes he may comfort himself with this, that he does not go off his father's territory. God's kingdom rules over all, even the worms of this earth are not below His cognizance, nor from under His dominion.

I want to say that I did not despise all the advice I was given-they are all good but I was only putting the immutable word to test, I was putting my faith on the unchangeable word to work. For the bible says faith without work is dead. And God's word is capable of producing result always for those who hold onto this immutable word, it cannot fail but produce for them. So until the word of God produces proves for you, there is no reason to give up. Only be ready to reason with God based on His revealed and inspired word. I reasoned persistently with Him on His word and a miracle was given birth to. God established me real good in that land. It is a testimony I will live to tell my children and children's children. Yours is next.

Beloved, the written word of God cannot change, the word of man is subject to change but God's word is ever sure. God's word cannot change in your situation but it will change your situation. You'll be glad to know that not even your sin can change the word of God. It will only delay the manifestation of the immutable word in your life. But in the course of time when you must have retraced your steps that which God says concerning you shall come to pass.

In the book of ***2 Chronicles 7:14***, God promised healing, the moment His people humble themselves and pray and turn away from their wicked ways. God is a merciful God; He does not change His good word concerning you. He will surely bring to pass, all that He promised. He cannot change. Your sin will keep Him far from you because He is too holy to behold iniquity. So that which He purposed to do in your life will be momentarily halted or delayed until the gap is bridged by your repentance. How long His word will be delayed from being fulfilled in your life depends directly on how long you remain in sin. All you need to testify of the immutability of God's words is a right attitude towards the word of God.

Let's see something in the book of Jonah. God sent Jonah with a message of doom to the people of Nineveh. When the message was delivered, within the forty days of grace, the king humbled himself, declaring a fast throughout the whole land. Both man and animal were involved. God heard their cry for mercy and change His decision against them; God declared through Jonah that He has forgiven them. One may ask, why the change? The word of God did not change here because; judgment upon a people is meted under a condition. What the word of God did here was to change their condition for the better that His word may be fulfilled in their lives.

You might have been a Christian for a pretty long time and now it seems things are not really working out. And when you check your prayer life, you are still in touch, yet it seems the word of God is working contrary. Hold on to your faith, God is still in control, He has not changed and His word is still immutable. Whatever you are passing through now is for your lifting, you are by those trials moving towards maturity. God wants you to realize that you are no longer a baby to be fed with milk always. God fed you milk as a baby Christian, things were going so smooth, your prayers were answered the moment they proceeded out of your lips but now you've got to grow up. You have to be an adult, get away from pampering. Realize still, that even when it seems abnormal, God's word is still unchangeable, it remains sure. As an adult, you have developed teeth (faith) in the word of God to chew (stand) flesh and bones (temptation and trials). Your testimony as a mature Christian will uplift a baby Christian to maturity, for you have been raised to raise others. Your testimony on the proof of the immutability of God's word cannot come outside or devoid of trials and difficulties, because they are the raw materials with which the efficacy of God's word is tested and confirmed.

David likened the word of God to silver tried in the furnace, purified seven times. ***(Psalms 12:6).*** The immutability of God's word has been proven beyond every reasonable doubt; it cannot and shall never change. The hard times you are going through is allowed by God, that by it your faith in the immutable word may be strengthened and you be taken to greater heights of maturity in the faith. Your present condition does not imply that the word of God has changed, His word lives and abides forever ***(Isaiah 40:8), (1 Pet. 7:25).*** Do not allow situations shift your faith on the immutable word of God, rely on it completely, it cannot fail. The only thing that will happen at the end is that your situation will succumb to the power of the immutable word. That situation will bow if you are bold to face it squarely with the word of God. You will surely testify of the immutability of the word of God in your life, if you faint not.

## Chapter Three

# MANIFEST IN DIRECTION

*"And thine ears shall hear a word behind thee, saying, This is the way walk ye in it, when ye turn to the right hand and when ye turn to the left" (Isa. 30:21).*

*"I will instruct thee and teach thee in the ways which thou shalt go. I will guide thee with mine eyes" (Psalms 32:8).*

*"My sheep hear my voice and I know them and they follow me" (John 10:27).*

Ask yourself these questions;

**WHERE AM I GOING?**
**AM I ON THE RIGHT TRACK?**
**WHO IS MY GUIDE IN THIS JOURNEY?**

You can keep your answers, if you do have any. These are some of the questions we need to ask ourselves daily as we go through life, yet many neglect them and abandon their lives to whatever fate decides for them. There is no sense of direction, anything goes. By His grace, since I was born both naturally and as a born again child of God, I don't do anything without seeking for divine direction. I don't move with the crowd. Do you know why? Because I believe in the total direction of God's word. I don't care if I'm the only one left. As long as I'm not away from His direction, I'm fine. His word declares His mind for me. The word of God is my only guide in my daily decisions and choice in life. And this has kept me on track in the journey of life. And I am determined never to part with the word of God. For whatever will take me away from God's word must have been able to take God away from me. The word of God admonishes us;

***"Let your conversation be without covetousness; and be content with such things as ye have, for He hath said, I will never leave thee, nor forsake thee" (Hebrews 13:5).***

Though this was originally said to Joshua ***(Josh. 1:5),*** it belongs to all the faithful children of God. This promise contains the sum and substances of all other promises. ***"I will never, no, never leave thee, nor ever forsake thee".***

Every true believer shall have and enjoy the gracious presence of God with him in life's journey, even at death and forever.

From such a comprehensive promise, you may then assume yourself of help from God. He has promised never to leave us, nor forsake us as long as we abide by His word. He is ever ready to lead us aright, the reason He has made His word available as our guide. The word of God tells us the right thing to do at the right time. If you can determine to make His word your guide, you can never miss your way in life.

Assuming you intend to visit a place you have never been to, it is normal to gather all the information available about how to get there. Thank God for Map quest and GPS. You need GPS and Map quest for direction to a place you've not been before. It is foolishness to set out on a journey to an unknown place without the help of GPS or map quest. (They work only in developed countries) Life's journey is likened to such journey to the unknown; we do not really know the way, no matter how smart we might be. That is why every Christian should seek divine guidance in every step of life's journey; we must constantly be in touch with the word of God to be sure of the mind of God as regards our daily decisions. Because our decisions as Children of God; should be guided by the singular aim of bringing glory to God. Many today are entrapped by the enemy because of some wrong decisions they made sometime in life.

David realized the importance of being guided by the word God, thus he said;

***"Thy word is a lamp unto my feet***
***and a light unto my path"***
***(Psalms 119:105).***

The nature of the word of God and God's intention of giving it to us is that it will serve as a lamp and a light. To help us discover the 'how' of man and God relationship. The word of God declares to us what we do not know, what is amiss or dangerous. It directs us on our work and way, and a dark place like the world cannot do without it. The word of God is like the lamps in the sanctuary and the pillar of fire to Israel. It is also a light to our feet and to our path. To direct us in the right ordering of our conversation, both in the choice of our way in general and in the particular steps we take in that way. It is so that we may not take a false step in the right way. We can only understand God's goodness to us in giving us such a lamp and light when we make it a guide to our feet and path.

King David was recorded to have fought many battles in life; he had a record of not loosing any one because of his habit of inquiring of the Lord before he steps out for any battle. He will always seek God and be sure of what God wants him to do before he makes a move. And one of the primary ways of hearing from God is through His written word, the bible. Whatever you hear and it's not based on the written word of God is not from God. For the bible is a complete and comprehensive record of the mind of God for you. Other mediums of hearing from God serve to confirm that which is already written. The day you decide to make the word of God your guide, mistakes on your journey will come to an end, you can never miss your way.

## HERE ARE FEW OF MANY REASONS FOR THE WORD OF GOD

- ***It directs us on the right way to follow***
- ***It helps us to make the right decision***
- ***It gives us a clear vision of our lives***
- ***It shows us how to live our lives***
- ***It is a lamp to that foot that doesn't know where to go***
- ***It gives light to every dark situation***

Are you in a confused state? The word of God is the light you need for clarity. Most people turn to men for advice instead of seeking divine counsel from the word of God. The bible should be our first point of reference. Because every problem or difficulty you will ever encounter in life, has a reference case in the bible. There certainly will be one of the bible characters or illustrations in the scriptures that will fit your particular circumstances.

All you need to do is discover the word for your particular circumstance and you will obtain divine direction on what you ought to do. And the moment you discover, you will recover your place in destiny. The advice of men might lead you astray but the word of God can never be wrong, it will always lead you right. Don't get me wrong here. I believe and I know that God still speaks through men but whatever man's advice may be, if it does not conform to the written word of God, it all amounts to thrash and must be treated as such.

The bible is clear on the subject of successes in business and other spheres of life. But many, because they want to make it quick and easy have resorted to herbalists and prayer contractors who end up misleading them, leaving them worst than ever before. You know always that the devil has nothing good to offer than steal, kill and destroy. Some, rather than obtain help, have been initiated into the occult. And it is impossible to serve two masters at a time.

***"No servant can serve two masters for either he will hate the one and love the other or else he will hold to the other one and despise the other ye cannot serve God and mammon" (Luke 16:13).***

The matter here is laid plainly before us: we cannot serve God and mammon together. Their interests are so divided that their services can never be compounded. If you are determined to serve God, you must disclaim and adjure adherence to mammon. The two cannot go together. If I may ask, who is the master of your life? I encourage you to make God your master today. He will guide you all the way and at all times. He will lead you safely to your destiny. He is never tired or worn out. He never slumbers and can never sleep. The Psalmist says,

***"Behold, He that keepeth Israel shall neither slumber nor sleep" (Psalms 121:4).***

God is a wakeful and watchful keeper, He neither slumber nor sleep. He never did, nor ever will, for He is never weary, so He has not the least inclination to sleep. He does not only protect those whom He is the keeper of, but He also refreshes them. He is always on the watch over His own to lead them to their expected end. He can only leave you if you decide to leave Him. The choice is yours.

So if you experience sickness in any affair of your life, all you need do is search yourself, to be sure you have not derailed and then find related scriptures to obtain divine direction for it. God has promised to bless the work of your hands ***(Isaiah 3:10)*** and His word is immutable. He also says that whatever your hands find to do shall prosper ***(Eccl. 9:10),*** and it is impossible for Him to lie, He would not have said so if He does not mean so.

God has promised to bless your business, yet this does not relieve you of your responsibility in running the business properly. See, God is a God of principles and whoever works according to His instructions testifies of His faithfulness. The promises of God will only cooperate with your adherence to basic business principles.

***"He becometh poor that dealeth with a slack hand. But the hand of the diligent maketh rich. He that gathereth in summer is a wise son; but he that sleepeth in harvest is a son that causeth shame" (Proverbs 10:4-5).***

Now, let's talk business. The scripture above identifies two categories of business people: the ones with slack hands and the ones with diligent hands. If I should ask you, where do you belong? You can keep your answer. You see, when you complain about business failure, you should also be sincere to yourself by asking yourself some salient questions. Such as:

- ***What time do you get to your business or work place?***
- ***How do you treat your clients?***
- ***Do you still treat them as special people like you used to?***

Though God has promised to bless the works of your hands, you can destroy the blessings of God upon your life with your own hands. Your attitude towards that business or your clients may just be the root of the misfortune you are suffering in your business. The scripture above says the one who gathers in summer is wise but he who sleeps during harvest brings shame to no one but himself.

You can recall that you used to wake early and get to your business or office quite on time. You were always on time to attain to clients, treat them kindly and encourage them to come again. You were increasing in favor with them and things were working out for you. But now, possibly you think you have arrived, no more propriety in business. You get to your business or office when you feel like, not when you are supposed to. Probably you expect your clients to wait until you come, as if they have no choice. I want you to know it now if you don't, that you are the man that sleeps in summer while others are harvesting. No spiritualist or herbalist will help you. Poverty is at the corner because you have used your hand to drag it to yourself. Go back to the word of God. All you need is divine direction and the bible is loaded with them. The recipe for your success in business is clearly spelt out in the immutable word of God. And Solomon says wisdom (God's word) is profitable to direct. Recall that God says:

***"This book of the law shall not depart out from thy mouth, but thou shall meditate therein day and night, that thou mayest observe to do according to all that is written therein; for then thou shalt make thy way prosperous, and then thou shalt have good success (Joshua 1:8).***

If you make the word of God your rule and conscientiously walk by it, you shall both do well and speed well. For it will furnish you with the best maxims by which to order your life. It will also entitle you to the best blessings because God has promised to give you the desires of your heart.

God commanded Joshua to conform himself to everything in His word and to make it his rule. Joshua was to meditate therein day and night, that he might understand and have it ready in him to be used at all times and in all occasions. Whatever affairs of this world we are mindful of, we must not neglect the one thing needful – the word of God. No man's dignity or dominion, no matter how great, sets him above the word of God. We must do according to all that is written, without exception or reserve, having respect to all God's word, even those which are most displeasing to flesh and blood.

## Chapter Four

# MANIFEST AS LIFE'S TOOL

When a carpenter wants to make a chair or table, there are specific instruments suitable for the making of the table or chair. Otherwise the result will be ridiculous. I want to state here that the word of God is an adequate instrument to handle all issues of life. There is no situation of life that is beyond the circumference of the word of God. Every situation that needs mending, His word can handle it.

You may be a professional in a particular field in life but added to that is your being a professional over those experiences you've had in life and the instrument of the word you applied and came out victorious. So what you need to do now is gather the suitable instruments obtainable in the word of God and apply it to your situation. As a Christian, you must understand that the word of God is instrumental to overcome every condition of life. You just need to discover the right word (instrument) that applies to your circumstance, use it and testimony is guaranteed.

A carpenter does not need an oven to make his chair and tables, it just wouldn't work. The oven is an instrument quite all right but it not the right instrument for making furniture. That is the difference. So when a Christian goes to a witch doctor to inquire for solution, he is definitely using the wrong instrument. You can only be a specialist in what you know. What business has a witch doctor with a child of God? A witch doctor will speak the language of witches when all the child of God needs is a word from God. How is it that you want to eat bread and you went to the hardware store? Of course if you go to a clothing store in search of bread, you are still at the wrong place and all you can expect is disappointment. Need I remind you that the word of God never disappoints, it has never been known to fail, and rather there is abundant provision for every situation and season of life? And I tell you, the day you discover the instrument in the word of God for your situation and apply it; joy shall be your portion.

I don't know the season you have found yourself right now. Are you in the season of lack? You have tried your best; still nothing is working out for you. There is an instrument of the word of God to deal with lack. Only if you will be willing to sit up, search it out and hold on to it. Lack has never been in God's agenda for you but there is a word of the Lord that can be used to destroy lack, discover it and use it. Use the word of God against that monster, don't just sit and allow the devil ruin your life. There can be no expectation without you on the word.

Permit me to say this also that as you are expecting to destroy lack, remember that God in His word only promised to bless the work of your hands. Implying that your hands must be busy, you must be doing something. If your hands are not busy, God has nothing to accomplish His promise upon. That is why Apostle Paul reminded us,

***"For even when we were with you;***
***this we commanded you, that if any***
***will not work, neither should he eat.***
***For we hear that there are some which***
***Walk among you disorderly, working***
***Not at all, but as busybodies"***
***(2 Thessalonians 3:10-11).***

Busy bodies are completely different from busy hands, so also are their rewards. He who does not labor does not deserve to eat. It is only the laborer that is worthy of his meat. The loiterer is worthy of his lack. It is the will of God that every man should have some work to do, mind it and make business of it. And that none should live like useless drones in the world. It is the command of our master, Jesus Christ that with quietness, we work and eat our own bread. We have to by some way or the other earn our living other wise; we are not qualified to eat our own bread. There must be a work or labor to keep you from becoming a busy-body in other people's matters. Christ admonishes us to be active in our own business and yet quiet as regarding other people's business. Do not be a burden or problem to other people, don't seek to be pitied, you are not made to be pitied but envied.

Do not even complain or try to hide under the excuse of "I have no qualification so I can't get a job". Do you know that whatever you have not worked for does not stay in your hands? Have you forgotten that our God is a way maker? Beloved, with the power in the word of God you can be fruitful. With the word of God you can create a need that God will ordain and anoint you to serve. Hold on to the word of God, it can change your condition. It is immutable. What it has done for others, it can do for you.

Look for something to do, make your time useful, you don't have much of it. Living in the church always without a functional work does not and cannot answer to hunger. Some get born again and begin to live in ignorance. They wake up in the morning and dress to church in the name of being warriors in prayer, sleep in the church and sometimes becoming a nuisance to those around him and a shame to Christianity. Don't get me wrong here. I am not against people spending days to seek the face of the Lord. It is a necessary spiritual exercise for every child of God. But when people decide to hide under that pretence to be lazy, it becomes a sin and goes contrary to the word of God. I will advice that we use wisdom. Of course God Himself is a worker, and a hard worker at that. From eternity to eternity he will still be at work. If He decides to stop working, then you and I will certainly not be alive today. And you are supposed to resemble your father in all aspects. During creation, He worked for six days and rested for only one day. Beloved get to work and God will meet you there.

The word of God is instrumental in our hands not only for battle but also for meeting our daily needs. It is only lack of understanding that has kept many Christians in the dark. You can obtain answers to every question of life and at anytime in the word of God. Search the scriptures, there are discoveries to make, there are treasures to excavate, there is gold to dig out and precious things to recover. What will turn your life around and make you a living testimony in your generation is right inside the word of God.

To make your search easy, you may get some help from bible concordance and commentaries. There will definitely be a scripture that addresses your problem. Spare yourself the headache of anxiety and regrets of ever becoming a Christian. Take your stand boldly as a child of God, make good use of the divine instrument-the word of God in your hands and you will be celebrated. The instrument of God's word is for your testimony. Don't despair in the face of trials and temptation. Even Christ, the son of the Most High God was tempted of the devil. That you are tempted is a proof that you are a child of God. It means there is a virtue in you that is a concern to the devil and disturbing him. The devil is trying to quench that in you. Will you let him? God knows what you are passing through. He is only waiting for you to act on His word that He has given to you. You can be sure He can handle it, yet you have your own part to play.

Every child of God has a level of ability in him. God has deposited these abilities in us that we may overcome situations. God has allowed the stumbling block there because He wants to use it to catapult you to greater heights if you will take your stand and not allow it pull you down. If you can face that situation with the instrumentality of the word of God and the divine ability He has deposited in you, your promotion shall not be negotiated.

Remember these words of encouragement,

> ***"These things I have spoken unto you, that in me ye might have peace. In the world ye shall have tribulation but be of good cheer, I have overcome the world" (John 16:33).***

The entertainment we are likely to meet in this world even though we are to proclaim peace on earth and good will towards men shall be tribulation. The devil wants to cut us off from the earth, and God designs by affliction to make us meet for heaven; and so between both, we shall have tribulation. Christ encourages "be of good cheer, Keep your delight in God no matter whatever is pressing and your hope in God no matter whatever is threatening, always rejoicing, always cheerful because I have overcome the world". Christ's victory is your triumph. Christ overcame the prince of this world, disarmed him and cast him out and still treads Satan under our feet. So there is no reason to disturb your peace because of trials. There is no need to be discouraged, no need to bring yourself down when nobody is bringing you down. Take courage in God's word and that problem shall disappear.

Until you do something with God's word about your condition, nothing will happen. The word of God is sufficient in all situations; a daily application of it will take us through our storms. Probably you have found it difficult to make time to study God's word, so then go for counseling, you have need of it. That is why God has placed His male and female servants around you as pastors. Talk to them. You can't say you have no one to talk to. They are chosen also as instruments of God to feed us with His word and mind concerning our lives.

God has deposited numerous instruments for your use in His word to meet your need. Act and work with the word of God, your problem cannot survive the power of God's word. Quit complaining; speak forth the word of God upon that situation, and your victory will be sure.

***"There is that speaketh like the piercings of a sword but the tongue of the wise is health" (Proverbs 12:18).***

Let your tongue always attract health to your life not desolation and hopelessness. Because in the tongue is death or life, poison or medicine, depending on how it is used. There are words that are cutting and killing, like the piercing of a sword, divide and cut asunder the heart. And there are words that are living and healing. Be wise and let your tongue be health. Closing up those wounds which afflictions of the enemy had opened up, making all whole again. If you can use your tongue wisely, health shall come upon your situation. Let your mouth be occupied and busy with the word of God, the instrument of positive change. It doesn't matter the nature of your problem- physical, material, spiritual, financial or otherwise, the instrumental word of God is sufficient. The book of ***Proverbs 18:21*** says,

***"Death and life are in the power of the tongue and they that love it shall eat the fruit thereof".***

If by our words we must be justified or condemned, death and life are no doubt in the power of the tongue. You can do yourself and others a great deal of good or hurt according to the use you make of your tongue. Determine today to bring life and revive your situation with the word of God. Resist the spirit behind your situation with the instrument of the word of God. Self pity will do you more harms than good.

## Chapter Five

# MANIFEST AS WEAPON OF WARFARE

Life is all about battle, an unending battle till death. And for every Christian, the battle line is drawn the moment you gave your life to Christ. And every battle suggests the need for a weapon, something that will aid the fighter in his strive for survival and victory. In the battle of life, many have employed several weapons. Some of such weapons have been known to fail. Some seemed to be effective initially but all too soon it was discovered they were no weapons after all. But there is one weapon that has been known, used and proven effective and dependable through the ages- it is the word of God.

The word of God is a powerful weapon against every kind of opposition from the enemy's kingdom. Apostle Paul in his letter to the Ephesians' church refers to it as the sword of the spirit. And tell me what harm a warrior can do to his enemy without the sword. A warrior who goes to war without the sword need not be told the outcome of such a battle. Without his sword he has offered his enemy the victory, in fact a cheap victory without sweat.

The word of God is the sword of the spirit and as I already mentioned, the sword is very necessary if not an indispensable part of the soldier's weapon. The word of God is very necessary and of great use to a Christian as he continues in the battle of life and finally succeeding in the battle. With the word of God, we assault the assailants. The scripture is the most powerful weapon to repel temptation with. You will recall that Christ Himself resisted Satan's temptations with "it is written", which is what I see as a model for every believer that knows his position.

Though some Christians choose to "play safe" overlooking the indispensability of the immutable word in spiritual warfare. To them, they rather put on the shied, helmet, sandals, breastplate etc. but not the sword. This is because they do not want to disturb their lives. Let the devil mind his business and they mind theirs. Ignorance, stark ignorance I say. Such believers forgot that the best way to defend is to continuously be on the attack. The bible is clear on this:

***"And from the days of John the Baptist until now the kingdom of heaven suffereth violence and the violent take it by force" (Matthew 11:12).***

The battle is on and continues till the day you are translated to glory. Another misnomer on this issue is the temptation to take up physical arms against a spiritual enemy. Isn't it absurd that men will gather only to be taught or led into physically boxing a spirit that is not visible to the human eyes?

The violence the bible refers to here, I believe denotes a strength, vigor and earnestness of desire and endeavor in the use of the spiritual weapons at our disposal against the enemy. It also shows what fervency and zeal is required of all those who design to be victorious in the battle of life. The kingdom of God suffers a holy violence. Self must be denied, the bent and bias, the frame and temper of mind must be altered, and a stop must be put upon the corrupt nature. We must run and wrestle, fight and be in agony with the enemy to get over such opposition from without and within. This, I believe is the violence the scripture intends to bring upon believers. Failure to act on the truth of this word has led most Christians to a state of despair and hopelessness. Ignorance has swallowed a lot of Christians to the point of no return. Of course the bible says:

***"My people are destroyed for lack of knowledge" (Hosea 4:6).***

The truth is that those who rebels against the light, can expect no other than to perish in the dark. Because ignorance is so far from being the mother of devotion that it is the mother of destruction. And lack of this knowledge is ruining to any person or people. The battle of life is as old as creation. From the day satan contemplated exalting himself above the most high, he has always opposed the light and fights tooth and nail to ensure he wins as many as possible to his camp.

In his frantic effort to gain disciples, he foolishly attempted to convert the son of God but he failed woefully by the sword of the written word. And since he failed, his next strategy was to plan the death of the only son of God. But he never knew and was too short sighted to realize what the Lord's death would cost him. I'm sure he has never forgiven himself for making the greatest mistake of his life, because the death he planned, that by it the kingdom of God may be scattered and extinguished ironically brought more souls to the kingdom of God. And any moment he comes across the redeemed of the Lord, he is put off completely. He is never happy and shows it loudly, by his constant threats and torments of those who have been redeemed from his chains. He has personally vowed that he will make life difficult and unbearable for the redeemed. But, again he has made yet a greater mistake, because the life we live now is not ours but Christ lives in us. And since he could not prevail over our master, Jesus Christ, he will never prevail over us, he will continue to fail. But for us, our victory over him and his cohorts is sure, that was settled several thousands of years ago. Alleluia.

***"For the weapon of our warfare are not carnal but mighty through God to the pulling down of strongholds; casting down imaginations, and every high thing that exalted itself against the knowledge of God and bringing into captivity every thought to the obedient of Christ"(2 Cor. 10:4-5).***

Our walk with God in the world is spiritual, not a walk in the flesh. It is actually a spiritual warfare with spiritual enemies and for spiritual purposes. Though we walk in the flesh or live in the body and in the common affairs of life act as other men, yet in our work and warfare we must not go by the maxims of the flesh nor should we design to please the flesh. We should understand that our battle against the enemy is not a physical battle but a battle in heart, in our imaginations, thoughts, which we must pull down. And this is done largely by choice than by force. Yes, victory in the battle of life is by choice. There must be a deliberate effort to crucify the flesh with its affections and lusts. It must be mortified and kept under subjection.

The weapons of our warfare are not carnal, they are mighty and powerful, this indeed through God. The word of God gains a great conquest in that, these strongholds are pulled down by the scriptures as a means through the grace and power of God accompanying it as principal efficient cause. Evidently, the conversion of the soul is the conquest of Satan by the word of God in that soul. This godly weapon handed to us as His children is greater and more efficient than all the weapons of the enemy combined.

## THE DEVIL'S WEAPONS

There are some subtle weapons that the enemy frequently employs against the saints. These are just three out of the many weapons the enemy use against God's children.

## FEAR

This is obviously the greatest, and most widely used of the three weapons against the children of God. Fear is of categories and of diverse magnitudes. There is really not any man who was at one point in time not living in the fear of this or that, indicating the far-reaching effect of this weapon of the enemy. But the word of God has an enormous supply of the panacea for this ailment in 'fear not'. In fact the number of 'fear not' in the word of God is more than the number of reasons man will want to give as an excuse to live in fear. It is disappointing sometimes that there is actually no cause for fear but the devil delights in seeing the saints in the cage of fear, so he manipulates man into creating the fear that does not exist. And unfortunately many do not survive the trauma of it. Now ask yourself for a moment, what are you afraid of?

If you stop to ask yourself this question, you may eventually discover that there is no cause for you to be afraid all this while. There is no cause also to doubt God's immutable word. If fear was just the absent of faith, it would have been milder. But fear is actually in the advantage of your adversary to gain cheap victory over you. When you permit fear in your life, you are merely professing that God is unable to protect you and that the enemy is able to harm you. What a slide! The word of God is immutable; child of God, your father cannot tell you not to fear when it will be in your best interest to fear. He says what He means and means what He says. When the word of God says 'fear not' God means there is no reason to fear and that means you are safe. By fear, the enemy makes you feel the whole world is crumbling on you, little things are magnified and your strength fails.

It baffled me one day to see a sister (title holder) almost jumping out of her flesh, yelling on top of her voice with curses all over the place. Do you know why? She saw a lizard ran into her place. Those of us from Africa know how lizards run around everywhere without control. This lady did not see a lizard. The devil immediately magnified the lizard for her just to put her to flight. Wow! If an ordinary lizard can create such a scene, I wonder then what will happen if she sees a snake. She might probably desert her own house for the enemy to occupy. Don't you think the enemy has an easy prey on such one? This might as well be the case of many Christians today. Little things can make them loose sleep and stay awake to bind and loose what is not. Don't let the devil put you on prayer marathon born out of fear rather than necessity. What you might really need to do is speak the word of God, a proclamation of the immutable word of God by faith upon that situation. Remember that all things are only possible to him that believes. And most times, the prayer motivated by fear is not a prayer of faith that the bible says avails much. There are actually some situations you need to confront face to face with the word of God and watch the enemy crumble. Fear is not in God's vocabulary for His children. The bible says,

***"For God has not given us the spirit of fear but of power and of love, and of a sound mind" (2 Timothy 1:7).***

Fear does not come from God; it comes directly from the devil. The spirit of fear is an evil spirit and an instrument of the devil. And anything that does not come from God should not be cherished or permitted by God's children. It is not to our good. Fear is meant to push God's children to their limits and force them to succumb to the manipulations of the enemy.

In ***Matthew 25:25,*** it was out of fear that the foolish servant buried his talent and did not trade with it. God had already armed us against the spirit of fear, by often bidding us 'fear not'. Fear not the face of man or the dangers you may meet with in the way of your duty. Reason is that God has delivered us from the spirit of fear and has given us the spirit of power and of love and of a sound mind.

The spirit of power, of courage and resolution helps to withstand difficulties and dangers. The spirit of love will carry us through the oppositions we may meet with. Just as Jacob made nothing of the hard service he was to endure for Rachel; the spirit of love to God will set us above the fear of man and all the hurt that a man can do to us. While the spirit of sound mind, will give us the peace that we need even in the midst of storm.

We will not dispute the fact that, most of the time we create fear out of our own fancy and imaginations, but if we are sober in mind we will obviate such negativity. The devil's condition is already known and settled. Against a true believer in Christ, his antics are but total failure. As such, any believer in Christ who is still living in fear needs a spiritual check up. And Apostle Peter admonishes us to.

***"Be sober, be vigilant; because your adversary the devil, as a roaring lion, walketh about seeking whom he may devour; who resist steadfast in the faith knowing that the same afflictions are accomplished in your brethren that are in the world" (1 Pet. 5:8-9).***

The bible says the devil is as a roaring lion. Note the word 'as' implying that the devil seems to be but is actually not. That means the devil is not a lion. He is like a roaring lion, hungry, fierce, and cruel; the fierce and greedy pursuer of souls. His whole design is to devour and destroy souls. To this end, he is unwearied and restless in his malicious endeavor, for he always goes about night and day studying and contriving whom he may ensnare to their eternal ruin. As Christians who are not ignorant of his devices, our duty is to be sober and govern both the outward and the inward man by the rules of temperance and modesty as encouraged by the word of God. We are to be vigilant and not feel insecure or become careless but rather watchful of constant danger from this spiritual enemy, and be diligent to prevent his designs and in order save our souls. We must be well grounded on the word of God, which is our weapon, resolute and steadfast in the faith, no matter what.

Maybe I should add that since the devil is not a lion, it might be true that he is actually a cat. He is a cat hiding at a corner with a microphone that magnifies his voice to sound like the roaring of a lion. And who knows he might even be a rat or less than a rat. And tell me that cat, rat or any of such that can stand the two edged sword, the immutable word of God? Child of God, the word of God is so fierce a weapon that the enemy cannot withstand. Our faith in the word of God can pull down whatever the strongholds of the devil might be. The devil's actions, manipulations and devices are meant to bring fear upon us. This is actually the point the devil wants to score. It is a pity though, because as for me, he has missed it. With the weapon of the word of God spoken in faith, I will stand and resist him and he has no choice but to flee. And of course we have the lion of the tribe of Judah who is able to devour everything that sounds like a lion.

## IGNORANCE

From the foregoing we can understand the danger of ignorance when the enemy roars as a lion. It is ignorance that gives birth to fear deflating the believers' authority over the devil and his agents. The devil is only a chief manipulator; he has no power when compared with the power in the word of our master. All we need to know is his devices and then with the weapon of the word of God show him his place, silencing him to a corner.

***"Lest Satan should get an advantage of us; for we are not ignorant of his devices" (2 Corinthians 2:11).***

Satan is a subtle enemy, and uses many strategies to deceive us, and we should be very cautious lest we give him any occasion to do so. We are to be vigilant, understand his operations, so that he will not take any advantage over us. Knowing that the spiritual controls the physical, we should be able to view all that concerns us from a spiritual perspective. If we can win our battles in the spirit, it will definitely manifest in the physical.

Let's talk a little bit about some of the beings we are dealing with. In the spiritual realm, there are active and dormant occupants:

- Active occupants: Here we have God, Jesus, Holy Spirit and the Angels. Also there are devil and his agents.
- Dormant occupants: Includes the saints in heaven, the chained demons and all the occupants of hell. ***(Dan. 10:10-14, 20-21, Col. 2:14-15).***

The bible is emphatic on the nature of our warfare with the enemy;

***"For the weapons of our warfare are not carnal, but mighty through God to the pulling down of strongholds" (2 Corinthians 10:4).***

We are facing a spiritual enemy which equally necessitates a spiritual weapon-the word of God. With the immutable word of God, our victory is sure. The kingdom of our God is a superior kingdom to that of the devil. It is the kingdom of light, the light that shines into darkness which the darkness cannot comprehend. The light is a master over darkness. ***(John 1:5).*** The light in God's word exposes the dark devices of the devil.

The devil afflicts through:

- Possession
- Obsession
- Oppression

The word of God mortifies and equips against any of these devices. God will always want us to be alert and vested with His words. That is why He has given it to us. Prophet Jeremiah testifies of this,

***"Then the Lord put forth his hand, and touched my mouth. And the Lord said unto me, Behold, I have Put my words in thy mouth" (Jeremiah 1:9).***

God knew the kind of opposition prophet Jeremiah was likely to encounter and in preparation for it, God put His word in his mouth to face the adversary. God did not leave Jeremiah ignorant and defenseless. He touched his mouth and with that touch opened his lips, that his mouth should show forth God's praise, with that touch, God's words were conveyed into his mouth to be ready for use on all occasions so that he will never lack words to confront and overcome oppositions.

God did not only put knowledge into his head but also His words into his mouth for these are words which the Holy Ghost teaches. Jeremiah was given divine ability to speak powerfully, and as one that had authority from God. Jeremiah was not set over the kingdoms as a prince to rule them by the sword but as a prophet with the power of the word of God. He was set over them not to demand tribute or to enrich himself with their spoils but to root out and pull down. He was authorized to read the doom of nations and God will ratify it and fulfill it, all these he has to do with the power of the word of God.

Equally today, God has given us His word that reveals all the devil's secret devices so that by His word in our mouth, we will be able to root out, pull down, destroy and throw down every plan of the enemy against us. Whether they are sorcerers or necromancers, witches or wizards, or even principalities and powers, by the word of God, we obtain an unchallengeable victory over the forces of darkness. And by the instrumentality of the same word of God, we are equipped to build and plant the good things that should be in our lives according to the plan of God.

The word of God is an effective and powerful weapon of warfare that paralyses the enemy and to bring into manifestation the plan of God concerning us. This then shows the need to make God's word part of us. If it is part of us we will not just speak it from our mouth but from our heart and it will be seen all over us. A man that is filled with the word of God walks head and shoulder high. There is nothing to fear because in event of any occurrence, you are equipped to detect it and where it is coming from. Of course the same word of God will also furnish you with the next line of action to counter the enemy's missiles. And the enemy will obviously be on his heels if you act in obedience to God's word. And this obedience implies submission to the counsel of God's word on the matter; such submission precedes our victory over the devil.

James admonishes;

> ***"Submit yourselves therefore to God. Resist the devil, and he will flee from you (James 4:7).***

Submitting ourselves to God also implies submitting to the knowledge of His word and accepting the direction it furnishes. If we are not ignorant of the enemy's devices and manners, it is impossible for him to have dominion over us.

As Christians, we should by grace learn to glory in our submissions to God. We must submit ourselves to Him as subjects to their prince, in duty, and as a friend will submit to another, in love and interest. Submit our understandings to the truths of God's word; submit our wills to the will of His precept, the will of His providence. Submit yourselves to God as considering how many ways we are bound to this, and as considering what advantage we stand to gain by it. For God's dominion over us will not hurt us but will do us good. We should not be ignorant of the fact that this subjection and submission to God is what the devil most industriously strives to hinder. So we ought with great care and steadfastness to resist his suggestions then he will flee.

## DEPRESSION

Depression is another arrow of the devil against believers. Many believers have allowed depression to swallow their spiritual authority. Troubles and difficulties of life make them to be downcast, forgetting the instrumentality of God's word in correcting whatever the enemy had spoilt. We must understand that there can never be victory without a battle. The trials of our faith are actually meant for our promotion. And God knows about whatever you are going through but has allowed it that by it you may be better equipped and toughened for the top. He is not keeping quiet but only waiting for you to act upon the word of God, waiting for you to put your sword to action and by it pull down the strongholds of the enemy. Jesus says,

***"Behold, I give unto you power to tread on serpents and scorpions, and over all the power of the enemy" (Luke 10:19).***

To him, that has and used well what he has, more shall be added. Most times, it is not that the power is not given; the problem is that the power is not utilized. God has given the power as promised but the responsibility to tread upon the serpent and scorpions depend on us. The power deposited in you as a believer becomes useless, if you refuse to act by treading upon the serpents and scorpions on your way. We are not talking about physical snakes and scorpions here. Of course you will be on your own if you see a real snake or scorpion and put your foot on top of them. Be warned!

One of the characteristics of the devil is subtlety; he is likened to a serpent. And the steps of a serpent are not easily detectable. Most often than not, it's even its stings that announces its presence. Most times the bites of the serpent produce depression and discouragements. But must we continue in depression? Absolutely not.

We are to exercise our authority in Christ over these serpents and scorpions and overcome them by the word of God. Do not remain in that down moment. They must surely come. Snap out of that moodiness and begin to release the sure word of God all over your life. Depression can only remain as long as you remain ignorant or refuse to apply the weapon of God's word. It doesn't matter how grievous depression might be, it can't withstand the power in the immutable word of God.

Remember that the bible says,

> ***"No weapon that is formed against thee shall prosper and every tongue that shall rise against thee in judgement thou shalt codemn. This is the heritage of the servants of the Lord, and their righteousness is of me, saith the Lord" (Isaiah 54:17).***

No weapon no matter how sophisticated or artfully formed, skillfully managed by the waster that seeks to destroy, shall prosper. It shall not prove strong enough to do any harm to you. It shall miss its mark, fall out of hand or perhaps recoil in the face of him that uses it against you.

The weapon might be in form of sickness, barrenness, failure, marriage delay, nightmares like eating in the dream, sex in the dream etc; these should not depress your spirit.

No matter the weapon the devil is using against you, I want you to know that none of them is allowed to prosper or prevail against you because the word of God says so. The bible says you have the authority to condemn them. When the enemy comes with his weapons, we are to counter-attack him with the word of God. Listen to this,

> ***"Wherefore thus saith the Lord of host, because ye speak this words in thy mouth, behold I will make my word in thy mouth, fire and the people wood, and it shall devour them" (Jeremiah 5:14).***

God himself says here, because you have decided to speak His word into your situation instead of being depressed, He will make His word in your mouth fire and those manipulated conditions will become wood that will be devoured by the word of God proceeding from your mouth, so those situations should not put you to flight. Face the battle with the word of God and you will surely overcome. God has decided to put honor on you and His word in your mouth so that no one iota of them should fall to the ground.

His word in your mouth shall surely take effect as the fire consumes combustible materials on its way. God's word in your mouth will certainly be too hard for those that contend with it. It shall break whosoever will not bow before it.

## OBTAINING VICTORY

The word of God is a wonderful manual that furnishes us with the recipe for victory in the battle of life. There are diverse steps and procedures that have brought victory to many persons and groups in bible history. But I personally believe strongly in an acronym I call the **"DFC"** of victory. They are **DESIRE, FAITH** and **COURAGE.** These three steps I believe are capable of lifting us over the valley of depression, obsession and possession and above the mountain of our circumstances and strongholds of our adversaries without stress. This model has worked for me and I believe it can also bring down the hand of God upon your situation.

## DESIRE

The concise English Dictionary defines desire as ***"a longing for".*** From this definition we discover that desire is very personal. It is not what one can do for another. It cannot even be forced on anyone. It is a matter of choice; it arises by personal decision and need. So if one should say ***"This sickness will only end in the grave".*** This can only imply that such one has chosen to die of the sickness. It is a matter of choice. Someone somewhere on this same planet chose to trust God's word for divine healing of the same sickness and was healed. To say it in simple terms, you cannot have what you don't want or desire. But those who desire are entitled to the satisfaction of such desires. To a great extent, desire which is an expression of a need is the starting point of a miracle. God in Psalms 37:4 promised to grant the desires of our hearts. Meaning that without a desire, there could be no expectation. But the moment there is a desire; God is able and willing to grant it because with Him all things are possible. There is nothing too hard for Him to do.

The Psalmist says,

> ***"Thou openest thine hand and satisfiest the desire of every living thing" (Psalms 145:16).***

All the creatures depend on God for their needs as they had their being from Him at first, from Him they have all the supports of their being and depend on Him for the continuance of it. The eyes of expectation of the creatures look upon God. The hand of God's bounty is stretched out to them. God gives them their meat in due season, the meat proper for them and at the proper time when they need it so that none of the creatures ordinarily perish for want of food, no, not even in winter. God opens His hands to satisfy our desires. We only have to commence the process by desiring something from Him. Anyone who is hungry should desire food, that is one step of victory over hunger and God will open His hands to satisfy that desire. When we play our part, He will in turn respond with the execution of His part.

Most times, it is not as if we are ignorant of the fact that God expects us to desire for what He has promised to bless our lives with, but sometimes something stands as a barrier. The bible says, even when we expresses our desire.

> ***"Behold, the Lord's hand is not shortened that it cannot save,***

> ***neither his ear heavy that it cannot hear" (Isaiah 59:1).***

Prophet Isaiah here rectified the mistake of those who had been quarrelling with God because they've not had the deliverance which they are fasting and praying for. It is not God's fault. He is still as able as ever to help. His hands are not shortened and His power is not at all reduced or abridge. No, His hands have not waxed weak but our sins have separated us from God. The moment sin is dealt with; we will be back on the path to victory.

Beloved, God is ready to help you. He is ready to grant you the victory over your adversaries. His hands are not short that He cannot save you from the afflictions of the enemy. His ears are open to listen to the desires of your heart and also to grant them. He is waiting to be invited into your battle, yes to be invited into that fierce battle so that He might prove Himself strong as the Almighty. Listen to what He has to say to you,

> ***"For I know the thought that I think towards you, saith the Lord, thoughts of peace, and not of evil, to give you an expected end" (Jeremiah 29:11).***

Doesn't it sound wonderful that of the trillions of people on planet earth, God is thinking of you? Your well-being, your welfare gives Him concern, He cares for you, yes, you. His thought are all working towards the expected end, which He will give in due time. Surely, you will see the end, the comfortable termination of your troubles, though it last long, it shall not last always.

In the midst of that battle, His thought for you is that of peace, He wants you to have peace. So, desire His peace and it shall be yours, Amen.

**FAITH**

Faith is an indispensable weapon through which we can overcome our adversary in the battle of life. Know it today; the devil is always afraid of the man of faith. It is only a man of faith that can surprise the devil. Faith is a sign post of victory in the kingdom of God. Faith is neither an ideology nor a mental condition, it is seeing with the eye of God. It is acting as God in the face of a manipulated condition from the pit of hell. A man of faith will search to discover what the word of God says about his present condition and begin to recover what he lost by declaring God's word against the force behind that situation and the devil has no choice but to flee. Faith has no room for sluggishness. A man of faith is bold and active. He does not surrender to circumstances but circumstances surrender to him. He is unstoppable, not by his power but by the divine power at work in him.

Paul said,

***"I can do all things through Christ which strengtheneth me" (Phillipians 4:13).***

All things here include every battle that might ever come our way. We can overcome through faith in Christ. Of course, it is only through Christ who strengthens us that we can make, not in our own strength. The divine strength that we need is propelled by our faith and our faith is motivated by the inspired and immutable word of God. The bible says,

***"So then faith cometh by hearing,***
***and hearing by the word of God"***
***(Romans 10:17).***

THE WORD OF God energizes faith; it is a catalyst for miracles. ***Mark 10: 46-52*** recorded the story of blind Bartimaeus. He must have been hearing about Jesus and His miracles. This fateful day, he heard that Jesus was passing his way. He must have said in his heart "God has buttered my bread." So he determined within him to gain victory over his situation with the help of Jesus. Note that this man was blind and could not see. He had not seen Jesus before as others had the privilege. He only heard about Jesus and by hearing, he believed that his victory was possible at that moment. He needed not to see how huge or short, fat or thin Jesus was before he believed. The words he heard were enough to build up his faith. Can we find such a faith today? Only be careful what you permit your ear to hear because what you hear has a direct influence on your attitude towards the word of God. What you permit into your ears can puncture your faith and leave you at the mercies of the adversary.

Many tried to shout down blind Bartimaeus but he refused to be intimidated by their shouts because he had a target.

Though he was blind, he was able to see through the eyes of faith what the sighted people could not see. He saw possibilities, solution, and divine intervention upon his situation. What are you hearing and what are you seeing? Is it defeat or victory, failure or success? Are you listening to the word of God or what the people around you are saying? God is waiting to manifest His almightiness as you demonstrate an unshakable faith in His word. Faith cannot be hidden but manifested. As you manifest faith, God will manifest His power to grant you an unchallengeable victory. This point of exercising faith is where most believers lose out. God cherishes and appreciates faith, it moves Him to action.

The bible, in a bid to emphasize the importance of faith informs us,

> ***"But without faith it is impossible to please Him; for He that cometh to God must believe that He is; and that He is a rewarder of them that diligently seek Him, (Heb. 11:6).***

Faith excites God; it makes Him happy and moves Him to unusual manifestation. According to this scripture you cannot please God if your content is faith-less. Without an active faith in our walk with God, it is impossible to please Him. Belief that wavers as the sea or wishful desire does not qualify as faith. Faith is substantial and it is the manifestation of the divine power in the word of God that enables us to understand divine things. Jesus while talking of the efficacy of faith said,

***"Verily, verily, I say unto you, he that believeth on me, the works that I do shall he do also; and greater than these shall he do; because I go unto my father" (John14:12).***

Jesus here was admonishing His followers what height faith can launch them to. And by the exercise of faith we saw the manifestation of God's power in the life of the Apostles. Christ healed with the hem of His garment, but Peter with his shadow ***(act 5:15)***, Paul by the handkerchief that had touched him ***(Act 19:12).*** Christ wrought miracles for two or three years in one country, but His followers wrought miracles in His name for many years in diverse countries. And I have no doubt in my heart that we shall do greater works, as there be occasion, to the glory of God. You will obtain greater victories by the word of God than had been obtained while Christ was on earth.

Evidently, all that Jesus did were accomplished through faith. If Jesus didn't have faith in His father, He couldn't have overcome Satan and his cohorts. And for the same reason He counsels us believers in Him that we might be able to overcome Satan. Remember that Jesus is the word made flesh. And it is only by faith in Him that we are connected to the divine power of God that pulls down all the strongholds of the devil. You cannot cast out demons without faith; the demons will definitely jerk the life out of you. Faith is absolutely inevitable, get it and see God working on your behalf.

## COURAGE

In the presence of desire and faith, courage is the motivating force to action that brings about complete victory. You don't have to allow any situation to make you believe, there is no use to keep believing God, no use to hold on or push ahead. I know we speak with human limitations sometimes, confessing that the situation we are going through is not easy to bear. Have you forgotten that you are more than human? You are a spirit with a soul enclosed in a body. Do not let the enemy pamper you to a life of defeat by self pity. Buckle up, pick up courage and march ahead. Remember, when you hit the bottom, the next destination is the top. Victory is by choice. You can choose to remain at the bottom or push your way to the top by your faith in the immutable word.

Know it that, no situation is more than what you are made of, for God cannot allow any trial or temptation that is more than you to come your way. So, the suggestion of quitting now is out of it, renouncing your faith should not be an option, pulling out will do no good neither passing the buck by trying to blame others for your misfortune, destroying testimonies of God's faithfulness. This is the time to take your firm stand by faith in the word of God and see what God can do. And He will definitely do something marvelous if only you will wait in faith.

***"Wait on the Lord, be of good courage and He shall strengthen thine heart, wait, I say, on the Lord" (Psalms 27:14).***

Those that walk by faith in the goodness of the Lord shall in due time walk in the reality of that goodness. Keep close to God, wait on Him by faith and prayer and a humble resignation to do His will; wait, I say on the Lord. Do not grow remiss in your faith on God no matter whatever you do. Keep up your spirit in the midst of the greatest dangers and difficulties. Be of good courage, let your heart be fixed, trusting in God and your minds stayed on Him and then let none of these things move you.

***"Be of good courage, and He shall strengthen your heart, all ye that hope in the Lord" (Psalms 31:24).***

We are not to faint in the midst of trials and battles of life, for they are actually meant for our lifting. Encourage yourself in the word of God, wait on Him, He will surely strengthen your soul. Whatever difficulties or dangers you may meet with, the almighty God, in whom you trust shall strengthen your heart. Those that hope in God have reason to be of good courage, and let their hearts be strong, for as nothing really evil can befall them, also nothing truly good for them shall be wanting to them.

It doesn't matter how fierce the battle might seem, God will certainly deliver us and leave us with everlasting peace. We should remember and bear in mind that there is nothing we are passing through that someone has not passed through and came out victorious.

Taking Joshua as a case study, on the subject of courage, the word of the Lord unto Joshua was,

***"Be strong and of good courage,***
***fear not, nor be afraid of them***
***for the Lord thy God, He it is that***
***doth go with thee; He will not***
***fail thee, nor forsake thee"***
***(Deuteronomy 31:6).***

Moses was telling the Israelites that as long as they had the power of God with them, they had no reason to fear the Canaanites. And though they were to be under a new leader (Joshua), since by circumstance Moses was not to take them to Canaan, they had no reason to fear because God is with them. With Moses or without Moses, God is Himself-all-sufficient. Instead of fear or trembling, courage was needful here that they will not give up, few steps to their victory.

The same applies to us today, in our wilderness experience and in the midst of fierce battles of life; we are not to lose courage. Of course God knows about our many trials and troubles and He has promised to keep us company till victory is won. He will not leave us on the way till victory is ours. Only that courage is needed to actualize a desire and exercise faith. Without desire, faith and courage, we will be defeated in no time.

Moses, while handing over the baton of leadership to Joshua, emphasized to Joshua the need to be courageous.

***"And Moses called unto Joshua, and said unto him in the sight of all Israel: Be strong and of good courage for thou must go with this people unto the land which the Lord hath sworn unto their fathers to give them, and thou shalt cause them to inherit it" (Deuteronomy 31:7).***

Though Joshua was an experienced general and a man of approved gallantry and resolution who had already signalized himself in many brave actions, yet Moses saw cause to bid him, "be of good courage". Now that he was entering into a new scene of action, and Joshua was far from taking it as an affront, or as a tacit questioning of his courage to be thus charged. Sometimes we let proud and peevish spirits stop us from taking exhortations and admonitions. His position and past exploit notwithstanding, Joshua needed courage that is motivated and powered by the word of God to face the battles if he must gain victory.

Having been encouraged, Joshua was able to also encourage the people.

***"And Joshua said unto them, fear not, nor be dismayed, be strong and of good courage: for thus shall the Lord do to all your enemies against whom ye fight" (Joshua 10:25).***

Having taken charge, he charged the people and imparted courage onto them because he was courageous. The victory God has given them over their enemy at that instance rejuvenated their courage that Joshua saw it as an appropriate occasion to admonish them that the victory shall not end but continue. Counting of our blessings can be a great way to pump up courage. Our focus should be shifted from the fierceness of the present battle to the power of God manifested in the past and which remain immutable. Focus on the greatness of God and not on the hopelessness of your condition. You need to be courageous knowing that God has not brought you thus far to abandon you. He will take you through to victory, no matter what. God has invested so much on you to abandon you without the actualization of His purpose for your life. Be courageous, there is light at the end of that tunnel.

Chapter Six

# MANIFEST AS SUPREME

In the order of time, in creation and over human government, God is supreme. And His supremacy translates to His word. The supremacy of His word is evident in the effect or proofs produced by His word. The word of God is given to us that by it we may overcome circumstances of life, surmount problems and rule our world. We have to stop magnifying problems over the efficacy and supremacy of the word of God. For in so doing, we make God seem impotent or incapable of accomplishing what He has purposed for our lives, we thereby make Him little. His word is supreme, incontestable and unchallengeable by the powers of darkness. His word is final and meant for our lifting above our adversaries to the glory of His name. The Psalmist declares,

***"The Lord gave the word:***
***great was the company***
***of those that publish it"***
***(Psalms 68:11).***

Yes, the supreme God gave His supreme word as general of the armies and the prophet as God's messengers were enlisted to make known His mind through His word. The supreme counsel of God as declared in His word, transforms our circumstances and life, catapulting us into greatness far beyond our contemporaries.

The Psalmist while speaking of God and His word said,

***"I will worship towards thy holy temple, and praise thy name for thy loving kindness and for thy truth for thou hast magnified thy word above all thy name" (Psalms 138:2).***

The psalmist said for thou hast magnified thy word (thy promise, thy will) above all thy name. God had made Himself known to us in many ways in creation and providence, but most clearly by His word. The judgments of His hands and greater things are done by them. The word of God is supreme and because of its supremacy, God has magnified it above all His name. To this end, the Psalmist once again implores God by His word;

***"Have respect unto thy covenant: for the dark places of the earth are full of the habitation of cruelty" (Psalms 94:20).***

The Psalmist knew that when God delivers His people. It is in remembrance of His covenant. So he pleaded to the Lord to have respect in His word even though we are unworthy to be respected. God's covenant cannot be separated from His word. All His word is an expression of His mind towards mankind. And even though the earth is full of darkness and cruelty, the word of God is not rendered null and void because God is a keeper of covenant. He respects His words so much that He is careful to watch over the covenant made in His word being fulfilled in our lives. Though the earth has been dominated with darkness and cruelty, the supremacy of the word of God is seen in the actualization of God's covenant with His people. And this covenant is made supreme over all the negative conditions prevalent on the earth.

## OVER SICKNESS

The supremacy of God's word is demonstrated over every kind of sickness, no matter how dreadful or hopeless.

***"He sent His word, and healed them and delivered them from their destruction" (Psalms 107:20).***

There is provision in the word of God for the healing of every sickness known or unknown to man. The devil, in diverse ways and times has harassed many with sickness, threatening them with death from such conditions but as such times, God sends His supreme word and the power of sickness is paralyzed while God's children will rise from their sick bed, healed. When Christ came to earth, many miraculous cures were wrought by His spoken word. He said words like- be clean, be made whole, and His words healed the soul, convinced, converted and sanctified men. In the common instances of recovery from sickness, God in His providence does but speak and it is done. He does it effectually: He delivered them out of their destruction, that they shall neither be destroyed nor distressed with fear of being so. Nothing is too hard for God to do- who kills and makes alive again, brings down to the grave and raises up, who turns man almost to destruction, and yet says return.

No matter how terrible the sickness was, Christ always demonstrated His omnipotent attribute by speaking a word upon the sick and they were made whole. ***Matthew 8:16-17*** is a testimony of the supremacy of God's word over sickness.

> ***"When the even was come, they brought unto Him many that were possessed with devils and He cast out the spirit with His word, and healed all that were sick: that it might be fulfilled that which was spoken by Esais the Prophet, saying, himself took over infirmities, and bare our sicknesses".***

It does seem that about the time of Christ's existence on earth, there seems to have been more than ordinary letting loose of the devil, to possessing and vexing the bodies of people. As such Jesus came with great wrath against the devil, knowing that His time was short. And God by His wisdom made it so that Christ might have the fairer and more frequent opportunities of showing His power over the devil. After all, the purpose and design of Christ's coming into the world was to disarm and dispose Satan, to break his power, and to destroy his works. The success of Christ over

Satan was as glorious as His design was gracious. He healed all that were sick, all without exemption, though the patients were ever so mean and the cases ever so bad.

Jesus casts out devils and healed the sick with His word. He spoke the supreme word over the sicknesses. Today, the same supreme word is with you to change your situation. So, confront that sickness with the word of God, apply the word, it works, make a bold declaration of this immutable word over that sickness, the word will work for you. For Christ has taken away our infirmities and bears our sicknesses. It is then our duty to confront sickness with His word and the sickness shall flee.

The word of God has dominion over every kind of sickness. So when you are afflicted with sickness, it is not a time to groan in pain but a time to speak forth the word of God upon that sickness. Even when you cannot utter a word, you can as well fill your heart with His supreme word. For the Lord watches the heart and not the mouth. Do not ever allow that sickness take your heart away from the word of God or the word of God from your heart. Jesus has paid the supreme price for our healing, so we have no reason to remain sick.

***"But He was wounded for our transgressions, He was bruised for our iniquities: the chastisement of our peace was upon Him and with His stripes we are healed" (Isaiah 53:5).***

Christ was in pain that we might be at ease. He gave satisfaction to the justice of God that we might have satisfaction in our own minds so that we might be of good cheer, knowing that through Him our sins are forgiven us. So, by His stripes we are healed. By the sufferings He went through, He purchased for us the spirit and grace of God to mortify our disease and put our souls in a good state of health that we may be able to serve God and prepare to enjoy Him. So the dominion of sickness is broken in us and we are fortified against whatever was favorable to disease. The name of the sickness notwithstanding, the word of God stands supreme.

## OVER SIN

Sin has been a major obstacle to the exercise of our right as children of God. This is because the boldness to stand upon the word of God is paralyzed by sin. Sin will make a Christian to slump before the devil and equally become a victim of the enemy. On the subject of sin, there are two sides of the coin. It is one thing to fall into sin and another to choose to repent of it or remain in that sin. The bible says:

> ***"Behold, all souls are mine; as the soul of the father, so also the soul of the son is mine: the soul that sinneth, it shall die" (Ezekiel 18:4).***

It is the sinner that persists in sin that shall certainly die. His iniquity shall bring his ruin. The soul that continues in sin shall exclude himself from the unmerited favor of God, which is the life and bliss of the soul, and shall forever remain under the wrath of God to his death and misery. The emphasis here is on spiritual death, which implies a separation or being cut off from the author and source of life. And apart from death which the bible says is the wages of sin, the bible adds,

> ***"He that covereth his sins shall not prosper, but whoso confesseth and forsaketh them shall have mercy" (Proverbs 28:13).***

Here the bible shows the folly of indulging in sin and excusing it, denying it, diminishing the effect of it or throwing the blame of it upon others. He that covers his sin shall not succeed in his endeavor to cover that sin for it will be discovered, sooner or later. There is nothing hidden which shall not be revealed. He shall not prosper, he shall not obtain pardon nor have any true peace in his conscience. By inference too, you cannot succeed in covering your sin because it won't work and you will not prosper in anything you do. Sin is a chief hindrance to prosperity. It has a natural attribute of attracting doom. Attempting to cover sin is a major reason for the sufferings of many today. And since the scriptures cannot be broken, many have been distanced from divine intervention upon their situation, due to sin. God definitely cannot reach out to bless us in our sins. Sin drives and separates us from Him. And the moment God is far from us, the next thing is that the devil will come closer to us because of the absence of God's divine presence. Failure to confess and forsake our sins will make the devil an ever abiding companion ultimately leading to destruction.

Most Christians fall into sin and chose to remain in it instead of rising to their feet and crying to God for forgiveness. They forget or maybe doubt they can be forgiven of such sins. They chose to remain with a guilty conscience and submitting to the afflictions of the accuser of the brethren.

The bible says:

***"If we confess our sins, He is faithful and just to forgive us our sins and to cleanse us from all unrighteousness" (1 John 1:9).***

Penitent confession and acknowledgement of sin are the duty and means believers are delivered from its guilt. God is faithful to His covenant and word, wherein, He has promised forgiveness to penitent and believing confessors. He is just to His son whom He has not only sent for the redemption of man but also promised that those who come through Him (Jesus) shall be forgiven on His account. That is why every confessed sin is totally forgiven by God, and He does not even remember them again. Problem will only arise when we refuse to confess and forsake such sins. The good news is that the love of God for man knows no bounds.

***"For God so loved the world, that He gave His only begotten son, that whosoever believeth in Him should not perish, but have everlasting life" (John 3:16).***

God sent His son to us that through Him we might be lifted to His righteous requirement. This He did on the platform of love, that through Christ we might be set free from the bondage and curse of sin. By His death on the cross of Calvary we are justified before God by His own righteousness.

The coming of Jesus magnified God's love, for in giving Him to us, we know now that He loves us. By Christ, God has not only expressed His dignity but His dearness to the redemption and salvation of man. Herein God has commended His love to the world. God so loved the world, so really, so richly. It is love to the revolted rebellious people to issue out a proclamation of pardon and indemnity to all that will come in. Though we were condemned for our sins, Christ came and took our place and by that we are therefore discharged and acquitted.

***"Being justified freely by His grace through the redemption that is in Christ Jesus: whom God hath set forth to be Propitiation, through faith in His blood, to declare His righteousness for the remission of sins that are past, through the forbearance of God"***
***(Romans 3:24-25).***

God, the party offended, makes the first overtures towards reconciliation. Christ is the propitiation, the healing bandage provided. Faith is the applying of this bandage to the wounded soul. So it is divine patience in God's part that has kept us out of hell that we might have time to repent, and get to heaven. It is by God's grace that we are saved. Our salvation is not of our merit but by the unmerited favor of God. Christ bought our salvation and paid dearly for it. Through the shed blood on the cross of Calvary, His grace has been made available for as many as are ready to forsake their sins.

Since Christ suffered all that man was to suffer, man is now freed to righteousness and not a slave to sin anymore. We have lost our former identity of sin; our identity now is to be that of our master, Jesus Christ. We have no part with the devil again. He has no right over our lives any more. We can now resist and over come him by the power of the word of God.

Those whom Christ makes free are really free. Because Christ gives a liberty that is true and certain, it is real, and has effects. None are freed indeed but those whom Christ makes free.

***"If the son therefore shall make you free, you shall be free indeed" (John 8:36).***

Let Christ set you free from the bondage of sin and the devil then you will indeed testify of real freedom.

## OVER POVERTY

Poverty tends to be very common in the world today leaving some of us desperately in need. The desire to make it big is a trend in the world today. The devil has enslaved many in poverty, so, in a desperate effort to break loose from poverty; the "get it fast" syndrome has found its way even in the midst of Christians. Some of us have misunderstood the fact that new life in Christ should attract some level of prosperity. And this is being misconstrued by some believers, who probably may not understand that the same bible tells us that there is time for everything. That you are not driving a car today or that you have not built your own house does not imply that you are poor. Do not allow the devil deceive you or make you feel that you are a failure in life because you cannot acquire material wealth. The devil cannot make you rich; he has nothing good to offer you as a child of God. He only wants to mess up your life and dump you. So do not succumb to his lies and tricks. It is the word of God that holds the solution to your present condition in life. There is no case that the word of God does not supercede.

God's good wish for us is that we prosper in body and be in health as our souls prosper.

> ***"beloved, I wish above all things that thou mayest prosper and be in good health even as your soul prosper" (3 John 1:2).***

The plan of God for us is that we should prosper in whatever we do. So do not allow the devil to put a poverty tag on you. Should you notice a sign of poverty in your life, don't be dismayed. It is not over for you yet. Here is the good news. The word of God has been given to you that by it you can create prosperity in your life and business. So speak the living and active word of God into your situation and behold a miraculous transformation manifest. The word of God possesses the capacity to attract prosperity and give birth to good success if you apply it, (Joshua 1:8).

The scripture says that:

> ***"The light of the eyes rejoiceth the heart and a good report maketh the bones fat" (Proverbs 15:30).***

A lot of us are yet to open our heart to receive the light of the word of God due to what we physically see presently in our lives and business or what the economy of the country is saying. In that dark alley of poverty, you should only receive and believe the good report of God's word concerning your life and business. When you receive and believe the good report of God's word, the business that was dry shall receive fat because the word of God has decreed it. There is no reason for you to be stricken with poverty when the word of God is available for you. There is creative power in the spoken word. So you can boldly declare to the devil that no matter the situation, you can never be poor. It is not in the program of God that you will be poor.

> ***"For ye know the grace of our Lord Jesus Christ that though He was Rich, yet for your sake he became***

***Poor, that ye through His poverty***
***Might be rich" (1 Corinthians 8:9).***

Jesus Christ, as being God, equal in power and glory with the father, rich in all the glory and blessedness of heaven, yet for our sake, He became poor. Not only did He become man for us, He became poor also. He was born in poor circumstances, lived a poor life and died in poverty. And all these were for our sakes that we thereby might be made rich. Rich in the love and favor of God, rich in the blessings and the promises of the new covenant, rich in the hopes of eternal life, being heirs of the kingdom. Jesus has taken our position of poverty that we might take His position of riches. So do not allow the devil intimidate you, the word of God has declared you rich, believe it and see it manifest in your life.

## CAUSES OF POVERTY

In the midst of the plenty that God has graciously provided for us, some believers can choose to remain poor due to some attitude they permit in their lives. Such as:

## SLOTHFULNESS

Slothfulness is one of those negative attitudes of believers, who even with the declaration of the word of God upon their situation can remain poor because God is a God of principles. In the book of proverbs 24:30-31, King Solomon recites/recalls his experience in the vineyard of the slothful.

***"I went to the field of the slothful and by the vineyard of the man void of understand; and lo, the nettles had covered the face thereof and the stone wall thereof was broken down".***

Solomon saw that unlike the rest, though the soil was good, yet there was nothing growing in the field of a slothful man but thorns and nettles. Not here and there one, but they were all overrun with weeds, and if there had been fruit, it would have been eaten up by the beasts, for there was no fence, the stone wall was broken down. Also these fields and vineyards are often in a very bad state, not only that there are no fruits, but they are all overgrown with thorns and nettles. The sluggard understands neither his business nor his interest. He is perfectly besotted. It is everlasting poverty and lack that thus come upon him.

Three things can happen to the life and business of the slothful as we can see from above. The bible identifies the presence of thorns representing harassment and troubles that will encroach into such a life or business. Nettles are also covering that business or life. The nettles probably represent annoyance and irritation as a result of the troubles the lazy man is encountering in his life and business. Thirdly, the stone wall will be broken down. Stone wall speaks of the financial security, the capital used in running the business. The direct implication of much trouble and irritations and that the capital of business will crumble. What a shame!

***"A slothful man hideth his hand in his bossom and will not so much as bring it to his mouth again" (Proverbs 19:24).***

All the sluggard cares is to save himself from stress and weather conditions. His posture is that of hiding his hands in his bosom, pretending he is handicapped and cannot work. When it is cold, he must find a way to hide and fold himself in order to get warm. And when it is warm, he remains in the same position. He hugs himself in his own ease and is resolved against labor and hardship. Let those that love work, do so for him. He thinks there is no such better life than sitting still and doing nothing.

He will not go through such pains to feed himself. He is not ready to take his hand out of his bosom, no not even to put food in his own mouth. And if the law be so, that those who will not labor must not eat, he will rather starve than stir. Literally, a folded hand cannot feed the mouth.

**SLEEP**

Sleep here does not imply the rest after a day of hard work but that which is indulged in while others are at work. Sleep is very essential to health but can also be a quick means of poverty and want. A man who sleeps when others are working to make their living has signed a contract with poverty and will rightly get his bargain.

***"He that gathereth in summer is a wise son, but he that sleepeth in***

***harvest is a son that causeth shame" (Proverbs 10:5).***

This is a justified result of the wise and foolish. Reproach and shame is for those who trifle away opportunities. This is about he who chooses to sleep when it is harvest time. It means doing the right thing at the wrong time. Sleep is good but the timing and attitude of it is what matters. One should not love sleep so much as to neglects his work, especially in harvest time.

Such one is a son that causes shame, a foolish son, who experiences shame when winter comes.

On the other hand, he who improve his opportunities, who take pains to gather and increase what he has, who provide for the future, while provision is to be made, the one who gathers in summer is indeed a wise son.

The portion of a man who sleeps while others are working is not far fetched, it is shame. You cannot prosper sleeping while you are supposed to be at your business. Nobody will come to your house to wake you from sleep; of course they have an option of transacting with those businessmen who are already at their business points.

***"Yet a little sleep, a little slumber, a little folding of hands to sleep, so shall thy poverty come as one that travelleth, and thy want as an armed man" (Proverbs 6:10-11).***

If men neglect their affairs, not only will they not go forward, they will certainly go backward. And poverty will come silently and insensibly, step by step as a sneaky bandit but will come without fail at last. It will come irresistibly, like an armed man cannot be opposed.

It is said that "too much of everything is bad". Too much of sleep can slowly put one back to mother earth, God forbid. But the truth remains that poverty is inevitable with such sleep. It will creep in little by little. And when the slothful is unable to meet his financial responsibilities they will turn around to surround him as an armed man and in the midst of it, he will be helpless. Beloved, wake up from sleep and get back to work.

## DISOBEDIENCE

As I mentioned earlier, God is a God of principles. There is always something you must do so that God will do His part. There is always an instruction to live by in every situation of life. Poverty can actually be dealt with by simple obedience to simple instructions or making use of some information graciously provided in the word of God. It is actually negligence to instructions that invites poverty and shame.

***"Poverty and shame shall be to him that refuseth instructions, but he that regardeth reproof shall be honoured" (Proverbs 13:18).***

One who is so proud that he scorns to be taught will certainly be abased. Yes, he that refuses the good instruction given him, as if it were degradation of his honor and an abridgement of his liberty, shall be overtaken with poverty and shame. He will become a beggar and die in disgrace. Everyone will see him as foolish, stubborn and ungovernable.

Disobedience to masters has brought a yoke of poverty upon many apprentices because they want to do it their own way, cutting corners to make it in no time. Forgetting that, the man they are trying to outsmart has been in the business long before them and has learnt by experience and duration. Do not let the devil deceive you and move you out of focus with ideas that will only end in your doom. Obey simple instructions, your master is not just your master by his personal design but God has a purpose for you being under Him at a time like this. There are things God wants you to learn from him, which will certainly help you in life and business. Take and obey instructions. God expects that you do so. It is by them that you can gain understanding.

***"Understanding is a wellspring of life unto him that hath it, but the instructions of fools is folly" (Proverbs 16:22).***

Understanding of God's word is a well spring of life which always flows and can never be drawn to dryness. There is always something upon all occasion that is instructive, and of use to those that will make use of it. And the understanding you have from these instructions will become an issue of life to you and your business as you act in simple obedience.

## STINGINESS

Stinginess is another highway to poverty. The law of receiving is that you must give to be qualified to receive. Human wisdom cannot explain this. Our natural senses will make us believe that by keeping and holding firmly unto what we have, we will accumulate and enrich our pockets. But the bible speaks in the contrary;

> ***"There is that scattereth, and yet increaseth, and there is that withholdeth more than is meet, but it tendeth to poverty" (Proverbs 11:24).***

Scattering here does not mean misusing or wasting what you have, rather it means sharing what you have; being generous with what God has given you.

The wisdom behind sharing is this; as the corn is increased by being sown, so a man grows rich by prudently spending what he has on charity and generosity. For God blesses the giving hand and makes it a receiving hand. Actually, a man may grow poor by meanly sparing what he has, withholding more than is meet, not paying just dues, not relieving the poor, not providing what is convenient for the family, not allowing necessary expenses for the preservation of the goods, all these tend to poverty. It cramps men's ingenuity and industry, weakens their interest, destroys their credit and forfeits the blessings of God.

By divine principles, giving liberally qualifies for increase. Withholding more than what is required results to poverty. A generous man may look foolish in the eyes of a stingy man. But the mystery is that a generous man can hardly be in want because those he helped in his time of plenty will naturally come to his aid in time of need. The more reason the preacher says:

***"Cast thy bread upon the waters, for thou shall find it after many days" (Ecclesiastes 11:1).***

In other words, do good to others around you with your riches and abound in liberality to the poor, it will abound to your account another day. Give freely to the poor, as that which is cast upon the waters. Send it on voyage; send it as a venture, as merchants that trade by sea. Trust it upon the waters, it shall not sink.

Give out, if you can afford to give much, be generous in giving and give to many people. Do not excuse yourself with the good you have done from the good you are supposed to do, rather, hold on to doing better. In difficult times, with the number of the poor increasing, let your giving be proportionally enlarged.

The reward of doing good to others is very certain. Though you cast it upon the waters and it seems lost, don't worry, you shall find it after many days as the husbandman finds his seed again in a plentiful harvest and the merchant his venture in a rich return. To the natural understanding, bread may carry the implication of waste because it dissolves when it is dropped in the water, which the preacher has this to say, "thou shall find it after many days". It is not wasted but preserved and enlarged. Receiving answers only to giving according to divine order.

***"Give and it shall be given unto you, good measure, pressed down and shaken together and running over, shall men give unto your bosom. For with the same measure that ye mete withal it shall be measured to you again" (Luke 6:38).***

Whether giving to God or to others, if we give in a right manner, God will incline the hearts of others to give to us. They that sow plentifully shall reap plentifully. For whom ever God recompenses, he recompenses abundantly.

When you give generously, men will give to you generously otherwise poverty will abide as a companion. Do not withhold generosity from the poor, life is all about sharing. Let's borrow a leaf from Job, who said,

***"When this candle shone upon my head, and when by His light I walked through darkness, as I was in the days of my youth, when the secret of God was upon my tabernacle ----" (Job 29:3-6).***
***"I was a father to the poor and the cause of which I knew not I searched out ----" (Job 29:16-25).***

God lifted up the light of His countenance upon Job, gave him the assurance and sweet relishes of His love. Such abundant satisfaction did Job enjoy in the divine favor and by the light of that he walked through darkness of doubts, comforted him in his grief, bore him up over his burdens, and helped him through all difficulties. God communicated His favor and grace to him.

We may look at Job as a type and figure of Christ in his power and prosperity. Our Lord Jesus is such a king as Job was, the poor man's king who loves righteousness and hates iniquity and upon whom the blessing of a world ready to perish comes.

Here, Job was giving an account of his life before his affliction. He did not forget the poor, he took care of them. He did not look on the attitude of other rich individuals, whether they were generous or not. He went all the way to do what he knew was right to do. And God for this other reason approved him to be faithful. That is why God did not allow him to die in his affliction. God was moved by his generosity that by divine benevolence he had double restoration of all that he lost. God wants you to demonstrate faithfulness in your own little way then; He will put a testimony in your mouth by His faithfulness. If you consider the poor and are concern towards their welfare, God in turn shall be concerned towards your welfare. Job knew the secret of giving and receiving and applied it in his daily life. If he hadn't applied it, it would not have worked for him. Most of us have shied away from the divine command of reaching out to be a blessing to others thereby inviting poverty into our lives and businesses.

**OVER BARRENESS**

The supremacy of the word of God is also manifested over the yoke of bareness. The word of God says;

> ***"There shall nothing cast their young, nor be barren, in thy land: the number of thy days I will fulfill" (Exodus 23:26).***

Probably you have identified an area of your life that the curse of barrenness is operating. The word of God says with ultimate supremacy that barrenness is not in the agenda of God for you. Being fruitful in every area of your life is a birthright in God. So, if the devil or situations around you is making you believe that you are barren, it is a blatant lie from the pit of hell. You may have been married for couple of years now without the fruit of the womb, don't worry, there is good news for you. The word of God which is supreme over all circumstances, is telling you that you are not barren. Your children are coming because God is preparing special children for you and they will come in His time. Remember that He never fails in fulfilling His counsels. All you need is patience. The insinuations of men should not depress you or take sleep away from you. They do not have the final say, God does. And whatever God says about you is final.

Do you know that some women, out of impatience have collected concoctions from fetish doctors who are responsible for their delay in child bearing? If you are a victim stop it now and learn to stand upon the word of God and hold on to it. It is only God's word that holds the truth about your situation and the same word says that you shall not be barren. Somebody gave birth to you, you did not fall from the sky and by divine order you shall give birth also to your kind. Why this will happen is that, men do not give children but God does. Men are respecters of persons and men-pleasers but God is just in all His dealings, there is no iniquity in Him. If any woman has given birth, someday you will also be a mother of children; it's just a matter of time.

When God shall accomplish His word in your life, the only difference between you and present nursing mothers is the time factor. As for children, they shall surely come your way because the supreme word of God says you are not barren.

***"Lo children are an heritage of the Lord: and the fruit of the womb is His reward" (Psalms 127:3).***

Children are God's gift. He is the one who gives them to every parent (Gen. 33:5), and if they are withheld, it is still Him who does so (Gen. 30:2), and that is always for a purpose. And they are to us what He makes them. Children are a heritage, and a reward, so should be accounted for by this understanding, blessings and not burdens. For he that gives mouth will send meat to feed it if we believe.

***"Sing, o barren, thou that didst not bear; break forth into singing, and cry aloud, thou that didst not travail with child" (Isaiah 54:1).***

You may have been tagged barren but the good Lord says you should not only sing but sing aloud and praise Him for He shall surely accomplish His supreme word upon your life. He has not forsaken you. Just continue in your faithful and cheerful service to Him, for faithful is He that called you and shall accomplish it. His supreme word shall surely be made manifest in your life.

The days are coming and we are already in those days, when those that use to know you as barren will come to rejoice with you for what the good Lord has done in your life. They will call you blessed because the lord has fulfilled His promises concerning you. So relax your mind and be focused on Christ, the author and the finisher of your faith. Your heart desires shall surely be granted as this portion of His word says;

***"Delight thyself also in the Lord; and he shall give thee the desires of your heart" ((Psalms 37:4).***

If you make God your heart's delight, you shall have your heart desires met. Do not only depend on God but solace yourself in Him. Just be well pleased that there is a God and that He is such one as has revealed Himself to be our God in covenant. You must delight yourself in His beauty and bounty.

This pleasant duty of delighting in God has a promise annexed to it, very full and precious enough to recompense the hardest service. He shall give you the desires of your heart. This is great. He has not promised to gratify all the appetites of the body and the humors of the fancy, but to grant all the desires of your heart, all the cravings of the renewed and sanctified soul. So take delight only in doing His will, continue in your service to Him with a joyful heart for He that watches the heart shall grant the desires of that heart even to the fruit of the womb. The word of God has said it, believe in it over your condition and barrenness shall give way to fruitfulness in your life, Amen.

Chapter Seven

# MANIFEST IN WORKS

Every word that proceeds from God is sent on an errand to accomplish a specific purpose. And God, from creation has been working with His word. Whatever God desires to accomplish, He does via His word. The word of God is always at work in the lives of His people. His word comes for a purpose and until that purpose is met in our lives, it cannot return to God.

***"For as rain cometh down and the snow from heaven, and returneth not thither, watereth the earth and maketh it bring forth and bud, that it may give seed to the sower, and bread to the eater: so shall my word be that goeth forth out of my mouth, it shall not return unto me void, but it shall accomplish that which I please, and it shall prosper in the thing whereto I sent it" (Isaiah 55:10-11).***

Now, if we take a look around us, we will find God's word powerful and effective, answering all its great intentions. And we can observe the efficacy of His word in nature. He says to the snow **"go to the earth"** and He appoints when it shall come, to what degree, and how long it shall lie upon the earth. He says so to the small rain and the great rain of His strength. And according to His order they come down from heaven and do whatsoever He commands them upon the face of the earth. It returns not without having accomplished its end, but waters the earth, which it is sent to do.

Also, in providence and grace, the efficacy of God's word is made manifest in salvation and preservation. It is in the same manner that the word of God, uttered by His children, shall not return unto Him void. It will not be unable to effect what it was sent for, or meeting with an insuperable opposition; for it is the declaration of His will, according to His counsel that He works all things. And it shall prosper in the thing for which He sent it.

This is the assurance we have; that the promises of God shall have their full accomplishment in due time, and not one iota of them shall fail. According to the different errands on which the word of God is sent, it will have its different effects and performances. One way or the other, it will take effect. God has promised that His word will not return to Him empty. The word of God is spoken to accomplish specific purposes in your life and no matter the seemingly impossibility or severity of the case; the word of God must surely do the work it has been sent to do. The word must surely accomplish its purpose because it is not the word of man, but it comes from God with a divine force and authority, making it powerful and effective upon whatever it is uttered for.

***"For the word of God is quick,***
***and is powerful and sharper***
***than any two edged sword,***
***piercing even to the dividing***
***of assunder of soul and spirit***
***and of the joints and marrow,***
***and is a discerner of the thoughts***
***and intents of the heart"***
***(Hebrews 4:12).***

The word of God is quick, is very lively and active in all its efforts. It is so quick, compared to the light, which is the fastest thing in movement that we know. It is not only quick but quickening. It is a vital light, a living word, it convinces and comforts powerfully. It is so powerful that it pulls down strongholds.

The word at work is powerful to raise the dead, to make the deaf to speak, and to make the lame walk. It is powerful to batter down Satan's kingdom, and to set up the kingdom of Christ upon the ruins thereof. The word of God is sharper than any two edged sword, for it will enter where no other sword can, and make a more critical dissection. It pierces to the dividing of joints and the marrow which is the most secret close and intimate tissue of life. Such a sword as this is a great help to our faith, to encourage our trust that whatever work or errand it has been sent for in our lives, it shall accomplish it.

The word of God does not only cut the flesh but cuts through the soul and the spirit. Meaning that whatsoever is troubling your soul or spirit will not be safe when the word arrives. Give the word of God a chance to operate and accomplish the work it is purposed for in your life. Remember that in the beginning of everything, it is the word that worked out all things. It worked for God as He purposed.

**HOW?**

The bible says:

> ***"In the beginning God created the heaven and the earth. And the earth was without form, and void, and darkness was upon the face of the deep. And the spirit of God moved upon the face of the waters. And God said, let there be light: and there was Light" (Genesis 1:1-3).***

You will agree with me that by the ordinary power of nature, it is impossible that anything should be made out of nothing. No handy-man can work unless he has something to work on. But by the almighty power of God, by the power of His word, it is not only possible that something should be made out of nothing but it can also be otherwise that some unwanted things existing in our lives can be reduced to nothing by the same word.

The earth was void and formless until God released His word. He filled the up the earth with His word, He did not use stones and woods to construct the earth rather stones and woods came to be as God's word was released. For six days, He was busy releasing the word, sending the word on errand and the word was made manifest and resulted in the reality of the cosmological earth. If He had not spoken, the earth would not have been. Today, some Christians suffer untold hardship and allow negative situations to prevail in their lives just because they refused to make use of His word. God has given us the same word that worked for Him so that it can also work for us. All we need is to grab this word, apply it and things will turn around for the better in our lives. Our desire should be to daily impact our lives with the eternal word. Making use of the word, of course is by choice, and not by force, but if you choose to apply the word, it is altogether a wise choice. The working of the word was made manifest in many lives. One of such practical testimonies was Abraham.

> ***"Now the Lord said unto Abraham, get thee out of thy country, and from thy kindred and from thy father's house, unto a land that I will shew thee: and I will bless thee, and make thy name great; and thou shalt be a blessing. And I will bless them that bless thee and in thee shall all the families of the earth be blessed" (Genesis 12:1-3).***

We have here, the call by which Abraham was told to move out of the land of his nativity into the land of promise designed both to try his faith and obedience and also to separate him and set him apart for God, and for special services and favors which were further designed.

God's word to him is that He will take him from nowhere to somewhere, from nobody to somebody, and from littleness to greatness. God changed his name from Abram to Abraham. Everything about him was changed. He moved from a land of scarcity to that of abundance. All these were accomplished in his life by the working of the word of God.

I have come to understand that before God will ever do anything, He will first say it, declare it, so that He will be committed to it. If it did not come to pass, then it is either He should be held responsible (no of course, He is a faithful God) or we do not want it to happen (which is likely). One thing is sure; God does not go back from whatever He says. When He spoke to Abraham, He went ahead to affirm the authenticity and irrevocability of His word by taking an oath of performance on Himself.

***"For when God made promise to Abraham, because He could swear by no greater, He sware by Himself, saying, surely in blessing I will bless thee, and multiplying I will multiply thee. And so, after he had patiently endure, he obtained the promise" (Hebrews 6:13-15).***

He swore by Himself. He stake down His own being, no greater security can be given or desired. God ratified His promise to Abraham by an oath. Although there is always an interval, and sometimes a long one, between the promise and the performance, those who patiently endure shall assuredly obtain the blessedness promised by the working of the immutable word. For every word of God is but a promise to His children, requiring from us a token of commitment for the fulfillment of the said promise.

You may ask, what are those tokens? They are; **walking with God, patience, and praise.**

## WALKING WITH GOD

Abraham was one of those men who walked with God in all totality. At age 90, Abraham did not see himself as one who had only but few years to live on earth but kept trusting God for the fulfillment of the promise. Many have denied themselves the blessings of God as promised in His word, as a result of trying to do it their own way.

Walking with God implies completely submitting our personal will to the will of God in every matter of life. It is doing so no matter the severity or difficulty involved. It is a decision one will never regret taking. A better attitude to this is to believe and conclude in your subconscious mind that God is a good God and can never lead you astray. When He called Abraham, He did not show him how far He was taking him, but the word of God was at work in his life. His end was indeed blessed. For that reason the scripture admonished us:

***"Hearken to me, ye that follow after righteousness, ye that seek the Lord: look unto the rock where ye are known, and to the hole of pit where ye are digged. Look unto Abraham your father and Unto Sarah that bare you: for I called him alone, and blessed him, and increased him. For the Lord shall comfort zion: He will comfort all her waste places: And He will make her wilderness like Eden, and her desert like the garden Of the Lord, joy and gladness shall be Found therein, thanksgiving and the Voice of melody" (Isaiah 51:1-3).***

Here, the people of God are directed to look back to their origin and the smallness of their beginning. Think of how Abraham was called alone, and yet was blessed and multiplied. Let that encourage you to depend on the promise of God even when a sentence of death seems to be upon all the means that lead to the performance of the promise. Look unto Abraham and see what he got by trusting in the promise of God and take example from him to walk with God, follow Him with implicit faith. He will make you fruitful, and so give you cause to rejoice. Your wilderness shall put on a new face and look pleasant as Eden, and abound in all good fruits, as the garden of the Lord.

No matter how long that situation has persisted or the gravity of it, a walk with God will make it right. You will be lifted above that situation. No man has ever walked with

Him and remained the same. If only you will not walk out on God, a positive change is a must for your condition. The Lord Himself has promised to comfort you in your affliction and you can be sure He will comfort you. Walk with Him; He will not fail to establish you even above your fellows. Apostle Paul said,

***"What shall we then say to these things? If God be for us, who can be against us?" (Romans 8:31).***

Paul was saying that God is for us, on our side. Not only reconciled to us but in covenant with us and so engaged for us. Who can be against us, so as to prevail against us, or hinder our happiness? No matter how strong or so great, even so many, so mighty, or so malicious, what can they do? While God is for us, and we stay in His love, and continue to walk with Him, we can with a holy boldness defy all the powers of darkness.

Let Satan do his worst, he is chained, let the world do its worst, it is conquered; principalities and powers are spoiled and disarmed, and triumphed over on the cross of Christ. Who then dares fight us, while God Himself is fighting for us?

No one dare stand on your way if God is with you. Your life shall be fruitful; no door shall be shut against you. The promises of God shall be made manifest in your life without stress. Sometimes we seem to underrate His greatness and might, by our doubts. Do you know that what you are passing through is not to be compared with the lifting God is about to bring to your life. Continue to steadfastly walk with God, there will be no regrets.

**PATIENCE**

It takes patience among other things to draw down the hands of God upon your life. For it is one thing to walk with Him and another to be consistent. Here patience comes into play. Patience is needful because lack of it will also deny you the blessings of walking with God.

You may have been receiving and claiming series of promises in the word of God or through prophetic utterances by different servants of God concerning your condition but it seems nothing is happening, don't worry, be assured that God still loves you and He is not a mean God. You may say this writer does not know or understand what you are going through. Of course the writer need not know or understand. There is only one person who actually knows about you. He is the one that can handle your present condition and He will handle it. There is no new problem on planet earth. Someone, somewhere at a time had passed through what you are passing today. After all, it is still the same old Satan; he cannot perform more tricks than he had.

This writer for one is going through different circumstances and eventually will come out a conqueror. There is no human on earth that is not going through one thing or the other. When you hear other people's story, you will look for a place to hide.

That this book is in your hands today is by divine programming and a defeat to the devil. I received the vision to put this book together since 1997 but the worries of life did not allow my mind to be composed enough to write down the things which the spirit of God laid in my hearts. The devil nearly ruined this vision and to make me feel unqualified. I was depressed and discouraged. But I thank God for His grace that was sufficient for me and made me realize that God does not use qualified people but He qualifies those He will use. You don't need any degree to be used by God. All He requires is your availability. When I received this conviction, I picked up courage and launched out to success. I encouraged myself in the Lord and set out to work. And God has proven Himself faithful since I began to walk by simple obedience. I resolved not to allow anything take away my joy again. For I know that He who has called me is faithful to perfect all that concerns me.

So, beloved, be patient in your walk with Him and wait for Him to make it beautiful in His time. He knows all that concerns you and He will do it in a way and time you know not, in a way that He will not share the glory with anyone. According to the scriptures, it was after Abraham patiently endured that he received the promise. Imagine that he was given a promise of being the father of many nations at the age of 90 years. One would ask, how many more years does he have to live? But before his death, Abraham saw all the promises fulfilled in his life. (To confirm that he saw his grandkids).

Do not be too much in a hurry, wait patiently on Him and you will testify of the manifestation of the word of God in your life, those who are mocking you today, will envy you tomorrow. Amen.

**PRAISES**

The third token that God requires for the manifestation of His word upon our lives is an attitude of praise, an expression of worship of His Lordship through genuine praise. Such was the habit of the heroes in the bible. They never allowed circumstances to imprison their attitude of praises to God. To them, God could not be compared with another.

> ***"Who is like unto thee, O Lord, among the gods, who is like thee, glorious in holiness, fearful in praises, doing wonders?" (Exodus 15:11).***

Here, the Israelites were expressing their pure praise and a high expression of humble adoration. Remembering that Egypt was notorious for the multiple of its gods, the God of the Hebrews was too hard for them, too tough for them and baffled them all. Beloved, God is to be worshiped and adored as a being of infinite perfection for there is none like Him, nor any to be compared with Him. He is the one that in all things has and must have the pre-eminence. That which is the subject of our praise, though it is joyful to God's children is dreadful and very terrible to His enemies. God is fearful in praises. He does not fear praise but value it because it moves Him to do the impossible for men.

Permit me to share this with you, in July 2000, I got a teaching appointment to coach some students in an after-school program, but after some months, the enemy tried to steal my joy by causing the termination of that program. To say the truth, I was really depressed because it really was an avenue for extra income in my life. Oh yeah! Big one, but thank God for His word. The word of the Lord came in the month of October and it was declared the month of ***"Heavenly Melody"***. So I decided to step out of my depressed mood and praise God no matter what. I refused to be depressed and the working of God's word was made manifest in my life.

On the 14th of the same month, the program was restored and my joy became full to the glory of His marvelous name. So friends I want you to pick up courage, stop groaning, it will not help, begin to count your blessings and be in the attitude of praise of God's faithfulness. If you did not remember anything, then praise Him for the gift of life. It is a good enough reason to praise Him. Don't ever allow the devil oppress you with worries and anxiety. You will only end up a loser if you wallow in worry and self pity. Begin now to praise Him anyhow and put the devil into confusion. Sing to the Lord for His is worthy of your praise.

***"But thou art holy, O thou that inhabitest the praise of Isreal" (Psalms 22:3).***

Praise is God's dwelling place. He is pleased to manifest His glory, grace and special presence with His people in the sanctuary, when they come to Him with their praises.

Then guess what will happen to your oppositions when God is pleased with you. When you praise Him, you are automatically giving Him the position that rightfully belongs to Him.

When you pray, the angels are the ones who come down with the answers to your prayers, but when you praise Him, He comes down Himself to accept your praise and bless you in return. I will like for you to give that a thought. The manifestation of the awesome presence of God in one's life is tantamount to the disappearance of evil and the afflictions of the enemy. Why not try praise today and see what happens to that ugly and unfavorable situation in your life. With praise, He cannot overlook you. Think of it, when you praise a fellow man or appreciate him for what he had done, he will naturally be moved to do more good for you. Try God with praise today, He will surely launch you higher than your expectations. His word shall be made manifest in your life and you will become a living testimony in Jesus name, Amen.

If you have been blessed by this book, write to me through my e-mail- jaclady1@yahoo.com or go to my face book page to like and comment on this book. Your candid encouragement will be greatly appreciated.

Thank you all and God bless you.